Alex Chediak's latest book is much bet... immensely practical, and deeply empowe... how paying for college works, how you c... money, and how you can land on your fee... want to waste a decade languishing in student debt, this is *the* book.

Zac Bissonnette, *New York Times* bestselling author of *Debt-Free U*

Far too many high school graduates take out college loans before realizing they have unwittingly subjected themselves to years of crippling debt. Alex Chediak feels their pain, and he has written a practical primer for helping to avoid the college debt trap. Before you head to college — before you even decide whether or not to attend college — you need to read this book!

Jim Daly, president of Focus on the Family

The author wants you to take college debt seriously — very seriously. After the first couple of chapters, you will feel you've been through college finance boot camp. But do not mistake the author's "take no prisoners" approach against unthoughtful college financial planning as a lack of support for college as a whole or for necessary college debt. After reading this book, you will never be naive or uninformed about the "why" of college costs or how to understand the financing of this important investment — an investment the author finds worthy. But you must bring, to use his words, "planning, grit, determination, and consistency" to the process. Once he asserts that poor upfront understanding and planning lead to some long-term remorse, his tone softens as he recommends college choice websites and demystifies government loans, institutional merit aid, and private loan options. His chapters on how to choose a major and how to make the most of a college experience, including through college jobs and internships, are right on the money. Every college student should read this advice sometime during their college career. I particularly liked his suggestion that students tithe and save from the get-go instead of waiting until that first "real" job. Lastly, his advice on postcollege life is what every parent wishes they could tell their son or daughter. The sergeant turned into the wise uncle. Good read. Worth every penny.

Shirley Hoogstra, president of the Council for Christian Colleges and Universities (CCCU)

Debt is one of the greatest enemies of the Great Commission. Alex Chediak knows the danger full well and offers a wealth of wisdom in this timely book.

Dr. R. Albert Mohler Jr., president of The Southern Baptist Theological Seminary

Reducing the cost of attendance should be a top priority for every university. Reading this book and following its solid advice should be a top priority for every potential college student.

Mitchell E. Daniels, president of Purdue University and former governor of Indiana

As an English and Communications major, I never took a math class in college. And I didn't think I could ever understand financial matters. But this book made it easy! Alex Chediak explains budgeting, loans, and finances in a simple way while also giving practical advice to help me be wise with my money.

Kellie Carstensen, North Park University, class of 2014

Follow Alex Chediak's sound advice and graduate from college with minimal debt.

Marvin Olasky, editor-in-chief of *WORLD* magazine

Worried that college may no longer be worth the cost? With student debt topping a trillion dollars these days, lots of parents and students are. So let's just put that worry to rest: Yes, it's worth it — and it's not even close. A four-year degree has possibly never been more valuable. But going headlong into debilitating debt is not worth it. The solution? Read *Beating the College Debt Trap*. Sparing no punches, Alex Chediak comes at the subject both as a student and college professor. He knows his stuff. If there's just one book you read about how to navigate the murky waters of paying for a college education, this should be it. I promise you, it's a motivating and inspiring read. Parents, give it to your kids. Kids, leave a copy on the kitchen table — maybe your parents will pick it up and learn something.

Mary Hunt, author and founder, *Debt-Proof Living*

It's no secret that today's students are making dumb decisions when it comes to choosing a college, paying for it, and deciding what to do once they get there. But no more. Armed with *Beating the College Debt Trap*, young adults and their parents can score a rockin' education without doing time in debtors' prison. Alex Chediak proves it's possible. Every teen and college student needs this book.

> **Lisa Anderson,** director of young adults and *Boundless.org*,
> host of "The Boundless Show," Focus on the Family

As a college student, I never had to think about debt. For most students, those days are over. Fortunately, Alex Chediak has given us an easy-to-follow road map on avoiding the college debt trap that is both insightful and fun to read. You will come away feeling both equipped and inspired. Best of all, he shows how the ultimate aim of minimizing debt is to maximize not our own wealth but our freedom to serve others in creative ways without hindrance.

> **Matt Perman,** author of *What's Best Next*

Alex Chediak does it again. He gives wise, user-friendly advice for students in high school and college (and their parents) for how to graduate from college without crippling debt. This book makes me even more grateful for colleges that do everything they can to serve students by keeping tuition low.

> **Dr. Andy Naselli,** assistant professor of New Testament and
> biblical theology at Bethlehem College and Seminary

Alex Chediak's book warns prospective college students about the many pitfalls and traps associated with borrowing to pay for a college education.

> **Mark Kantrowitz,** senior vice president
> and publisher at Edvisors.com

As a parent with two teens just starting college, I can't describe how thankful I am for this timely book and its beautiful but rare balance of realistic optimism. I pray that many students (and parents) will use this book not only to avoid the multiple college debt traps that have ensnared so many unsuspecting victims but also to make the decisions that will help students to thrive in every way.

> **David Murray,** professor at Puritan Reformed Theological
> Seminary, pastor at Grand Rapids Free Reformed
> Church, and author of *Jesus on Every Page*

Alex has given us an indispensable field guide to escaping the insanity of the current college debt problem. A treasure trove of practical wisdom and tactics. This is going on my must-read list for our church's youth and parent ministry.

Matt Heerema, pastor of Stonebrook Church

Alex has gifted us with a great resource for college students and parents—to realistically tackle their financial future and be mindful of the life God has in store for them.

Laurie Polich Short, author of *Finding Faith in the Dark*

A college education with little or no debt—the seemingly impossible dream for today's students. Here's how to make it happen.

Dr. Peter W. Wood, president of the
National Association of Scholars

With the cost of higher education going up far faster than the rate of inflation, it's easy for a student to take on crippling debt for no good reason. Alex Chediak has done the detailed research, thought long and hard about this problem, and provides an accessible and trustworthy guide for getting the most bang for the buck. If you are a current or future college student, or a parent of such a student, you owe it to yourself, and to your wallet, to read this book. I'm one such parent, and I plan to take his advice.

Jay W. Richards, PhD, *New York Times* bestselling author and
assistant research professor at The Catholic University of America

Beating the College Debt Trap is a strong, practical guide for thinking wisely through the significant questions about college, career, and vocation. The message is that these decisions are pre-life decisions, not just pre-wealth decisions. Alex's book makes a strong contribution to the college and career discussion and is a worthy read for teenagers and their parents, as well as for teachers and guidance counselors. It would be highly effective as a classroom guide for high schools.

Derek Keenan, EdD, vice president of academic affairs
at the Association of Christian Schools International

After writing for college students (*Thriving at College*) and for parents of prospective college students (*Preparing Your Teens for College*), Alex Chediak has now written a book that all of us need. Readers can trust Alex. He knows the college world inside out (both as a student and as a professor), and he is able to cut through the confusion, break down what you need to know, and present the results in a wise and accessible way. Learning the information in this book is an exercise in stewardship. Ignore it at your own risk!

> **Justin Taylor,** blogger and managing editor of *The ESV Study Bible*

A persistent myth exists in America that a college degree is a golden ticket to a successful future. If this were ever true, it surely is no longer. As a college professor, I believe wholeheartedly in the value and wisdom of obtaining a college education, but not without asking the kinds of questions Alex Chediak addresses in *Beating the College Debt Trap*. I urge every prospective college student—as well as every parent of a prospective college student—to read this book.

> **Karen Swallow Prior,** PhD, author of *Fierce Convictions: The Extraordinary Life of Hannah More: Poet, Reformer, Abolitionist*

From the foolish (using student loans to buy a boat) to the sad (potential missionaries having to stay home), college debt is a big deal. As someone who has ministered to college students for more than a decade, I highly recommend this book.

> **Jonathan Saunders,** director of campus ministry at University Reformed Church in East Lansing, Michigan

BEATING THE
COLLEGE
DEBT TRAP

Getting a Degree
Without Going Broke

ALEX CHEDIAK

ZONDERVAN

Beating the College Debt Trap
Copyright © 2015 by Juan Alexander Chediak

Requests for information should be addressed to:
Zondervan, 3900 *Sparks Dr. SE, Grand Rapids, Michigan 49546*

Library of Congress Cataloging-in-Publication Data

Names: Chediak, Alex. | Chediak, Alex.
Title: Beating the college debt trap : getting a degree without going broke /
    Alex Chediak, Alex Chediak.
Description: Grand Rapids, MI : Zondervan, 2015.
Identifiers: LCCN 2015032324 | ISBN 9780310337423 (paperback) |
    ISBN 9780310337430 (ebook) | ISBN 9780310066989 (mobile app)
Subjects: LCSH: College costs—United States. | Finance, Personal—United States. |
    Education, Higher—United States—Finance. | Christian college students—Religious
    life.
Classification: LCC LB2342 .C42 2015 | DDC 378.3/8—dc23 LC record available at
    http://lccn.loc.gov/2015032324

Cover design: *Dual Identity*
Cover photos: ©Henrik5000 / ©4x6 / iStockphoto®
Interior design: *Kait Lamphere*

First printing October 2015 / Printed in the United States of America

To college students,
and to those who will be or should be but can't see a way:
May you experience financial freedom
so that you can give yourself fully
to the good works for which God is preparing you.

CONTENTS

Part 3
Taking Charge
Earning and Managing Your Money

Part 4
Keeping It Going
Succeeding after College

CHECKLIST FOR GETTING A DEGREE WITHOUT GOING BROKE

☐ **1.** Save what you can in advance. If you save money before college, the power of compound interest works *for* you, producing a larger wad of cash with which to pay college costs. If you borrow money during college, compound interest works *against* you, as you have to pay back more than what you borrowed.

☐ **2.** Know as much as you can about yourself and your chosen major before going to college. This awareness can help you avoid needless and expensive delays on the path to graduation. And it can motivate you to make the right professional moves *during* college to enhance your success *after* college.

☐ **3.** Try to get your first year's worth of credits debt-free (using AP or IB classes, community college, CLEP testing, less expensive online courses, and prior savings). If that's not possible, limit yourself to no more than the *subsidized* federal loan (see Trap 5).

☐ **4.** Don't take out $10–$15K of loans each year just to say you attended a prestigious university. Instead, pick an affordable school of reasonable quality that accepts you (see Trap 3). Websites like CollegeData (www.collegedata.com) and the NCES College Navigator (www.nces.ed.gov/collegenavigator/) let you compare the generosity and affordability of different colleges. Apply for financial aid early in the financial aid application cycle. With regard to quality, consider the college's academic facilities, the availability of faculty, the rigor of their courses, and the school's relationship with prospective employers. Look at what the college offers in the way of Career Services and whether they have a co-op program (discussed in Trap 6).

☐ **5.** Alternatively, accumulate credits at multiple colleges (for example, by starting at a community college). But try to avoid taking duplicate classes or losing time waiting for specific classes. Depending on the sequence of courses required for your major at the four-year college to which you plan to transfer, you may need just as much time to graduate (if course A is a prerequisite for course B, which is a prerequisite for course C, and so on).

☐ **6.** Consider whether your parents or other relatives can contribute a donation or an interest-free loan to help with your college expenses. Go there before going to the government.

☐ **7.** Delay any unsubsidized loans until the last year or two, when graduation is clearly in sight. Avoid borrowing *more than half* your anticipated salary and stay below the cumulative limit on federal loans. Yes, this is possible!

☐ **8.** Avoid private loans like the plague!

PREFACE
WHY THIS BOOK?

Families everywhere are falling behind as the cost of living rises faster than take-home pay. The job market for those with only a high school degree keeps shrinking, while the price tag for a college education keeps growing. In the last few years, I've met countless would-be college students who have no idea if it's even possible to earn a degree on their budgets. I've also met dozens of graduates with frighteningly high debt loads. Their stories are variations on a common theme: "I wish I had known what I was getting myself into. Why didn't anyone explain this stuff to me?"

There are a bazillion books out there for midcareer men and women on making money, getting ahead, planning for retirement, and all the rest. But who is writing to *you* about the largest expense you've ever faced? How you pay for college will have massive, enduring consequences, yet so many students go into it blind. It doesn't help that the process is anything but straightforward, with complicated forms to complete, deadlines to keep track of, contradictory advice about where to find money, and students paying vastly different prices to attend the same school.

I wrote this book to help you cut through the fog and become a savvy, informed customer. That's how you'll get the most value for your dollar.

Beating the College Debt Trap is for any college student, whether

- attending full-time or part-time
- living on campus or off campus or taking classes online
- eighteen to twenty-three years old or older
- working while going to school or not

- enrolled in a four-year academic program, learning a skilled trade, or earning an associate's degree

"College" does not have to mean "four-year college." If you know you need additional training to succeed in the workforce — a certificate program, a trade school, a two-year college, something — but aren't sure how you'll pay for it, this book is for you. If you want to understand what the nice person in the financial aid office is talking about *before* you sign the papers, this book is for you.

Beating the College Debt Trap is for anyone who wants to get the training they need to get a degree without going broke. You don't have to be stuck in neutral because your parents aren't rich. You don't have to take on a mountain of debt just to have a shot at a decent future. You don't have to spend the rest of your life in a dead-end job. Join me, and let's beat the college debt trap.

INTRODUCTION

TAKE OWNERSHIP OF YOUR FINANCIAL FUTURE

Emily did everything right. She finished high school with a 3.6 GPA, was active in youth group, and applied to colleges on time. She was accepted into three good schools, including her top choice. Her family isn't what you'd call "rich," but they didn't qualify for government subsidized loans either. The good news is that Emily was awarded a scholarship to play in the college's orchestra and was approved for ten hours per week of work-study.

Emily's college was a ten-minute drive from her Uncle Chris and Aunt Jennifer's home. They offered her a room in their house, but Emily wanted to experience living on campus. She's glad she did, because she made some amazing friends.

But when it all got added up—tuition, fees, room, board, text-books, and supplies—Emily's family didn't always have enough, so she ended up taking out about $5,000 in loans each year. Emily was initially nervous, but the financial aid office made everything easy.

A few months after graduating, she landed a full-time job in the city. She was super-excited! Her starting salary would be $40,000. Not as much as she had hoped for, but a typical starting figure for someone with her degree that year. After payroll deductions and tithing, she'd be taking home about $2,150 per month.[1]

But then Emily began to think about how far that money would go. Her job would be too far from her parents' house, so she'd need a place to live. Maybe with a roommate she could keep her share of the rent and utilities under $1,000 per month. She estimated $400 per month toward her car expenses (insurance, gas, and oil changes or whatever).

Maybe another $400 for food, $100 for clothes, $50 for household supplies or personal items, and $100 for phone and Internet charges.

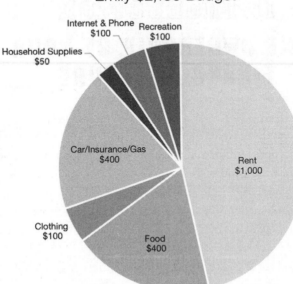

Emily $2,150 Budget

That left only $100 per month for going out with her friends. What about a bed and some other furniture? What about the traveling she hoped to do next summer? And what about catching a flight that fall to Megan's wedding in Chicago?

The arrival of the mail interrupted her thoughts. *Oh no. It's something about my student loans.* Scanning to the bottom, Emily's eyes grew big, and her heart sank. Her minimum payment was $250 per month—every month for the next ten years.

She started to panic.

College: Important, But Expensive

You're probably being told that a college degree has never been more important than it is today. So you want to go—or at least your parents are telling you to go. You don't want to be out in the cold, looking for a decent paying job when everyone else has a college degree. But how on earth are you going to pay for it?

Perhaps you're already feeling the squeeze of student loans. You've taken out $20,000, $40,000, maybe more. A former student of mine graduated with $80,000 in debt and then took on extra loans to pursue graduate school. Another has ten different loans totaling $90,000. His minimum monthly payment is $1,045.

It's triple jeopardy these days: College is more important than ever, less affordable than ever, and graduates have more debt than ever.

What's at stake here? Nothing less than the rest of your life. Going to college is the most expensive decision you've ever made. The consequences of how you pay for it will be with you into your twenties, thirties, and beyond. Will you be able to take that dream job you'd love to have but that doesn't pay well? Buy a house someday? Get married? Start having kids? Stay home with your kids? Start a business? Leave for the mission field? *Today* you either set yourself up for success or failure. Freedom or bondage. Peace or stress. You decide.

Most people borrow money to pay for college. Some borrow gobs of it. Seven out of ten college students graduated in 2014 with an average debt of $33,000, a figure that has almost doubled in the last twenty years, even after adjusting for inflation.[2] More than one in three student credit card holders rack up additional debt by not paying their monthly balances in full.[3]

I know. It'd be super-easy to throw your hands in the air and say, "What choice do I have? I have to go to college. Sure, some people have rich parents who can afford to pay it all. But I don't. My parents are maxed out. Tuition is expensive. Room and board are expensive. Books are way too expensive. I need my car on campus, and gas is expensive. Of course I'll need to borrow a ton of money. Isn't that normal? My high school guidance counselor, the nice lady at the financial aid office, *everyone* has assured me that I'll be OK. When I get out, I'll be making good money, and I'll be able to pay it all off."

> **It's triple jeopardy these days: College is more important than ever, less affordable than ever, and graduates have more debt than ever.**

A Better Way to Do College

A better way to do college begins with taking full responsibility for your financial decisions — past, present, and future. This may be obvious to you. You already know that paying for college isn't your parents' problem or the government's problem. It's yours, baby. But even if Mom, Dad, Grandpa, and Grandma are helping you — a little or a lot — it's still crucial that you own it — that you examine how much things cost, that you make careful, informed decisions because this is *your* life we're talking about. And it's the season to wean yourself from their financial provision.

If your parents specify how much they can afford to spend on your college experience, respect it. Don't ask for more; thank them for being willing to help you at all. And please don't ask *them* to take out a loan when their golden years are just around the corner. What if they get sick and have to stop working? Before asking them to risk their financial future, ask yourself if you've considered all the ways you can either spend less or earn more.

By the time we're done, you'll know how to make a budget and how to keep track of where your money is going. You'll know how to spend less of it and make more of it. Yes, college can be expensive, but diligence leads to wealth (Proverbs 10:4), and hard work leads to independence (1 Thessalonians 4:11 – 12). Students who contribute to the expense of college appreciate it more. They take school more seriously and become more financially responsible, which prepares them for life after college.

Perhaps you're thinking, *It's not my fault that college is out-of-control expensive!* No, it's not. But there are lots of things in life that aren't fair. Successful people recognize reality for what it is and find a way to make the best of difficult situations. They don't shift the blame, make excuses, or expect someone else to do what they should do for themselves.

Debt Is Bondage

Though many students now take out loads of loans to pay for college, this strategy lacks historical precedence, and we've yet to see the societal repercussions. For example, what would have happened if Emily couldn't find a $40,000-per-year job when she graduated? A May 2013 survey from McKinsey & Company reported that more than four in ten graduates described their employment as a job that doesn't require a four-year degree.[4] Yet they must still repay their student loans.

The wisdom of Solomon offers this nugget: "The rich rule over the poor, and the borrower is slave to the lender" (Proverbs 22:7). When you accept a loan, it feels like you're getting free money. You're allowed to enjoy things today on the promise that you'll be able to pay for them tomorrow. But what if you can't? It's wicked to borrow and not repay (Psalm 37:21; Romans 13:7).

It's also stupid, because the banks end up sticking you with late fees on top of the interest. So it ends up costing a fortune. For example, the $5,000 Emily took out in loans each year did not come to $20,000 after four years. It was more like $23,000. That's because interest was accruing each year. And if she fails to make on-time payments, late fees will jack up the balance even higher.

When faced with the high cost of college and a lack of money, it's easy to conclude that student loans are the most logical option — perhaps the only option. But there are downsides to taking on debt, especially at the beginning, when your major, job prospects, and graduation date can (and often do) change. Some loans pay the interest for you while you're in school, but *all* of them require repayment with interest after graduation.[5] *All* of them limit your freedom to pursue your dreams. And *all* of them can lead to unbelievable stress. Six out of ten current students and recent graduates worry they won't be able to pay off their loans before their thirtieth birthday.[6] Is that how you imagined life after college?

The Dangers of Student Loan Debt

Some Christians think debt is never permissible, because of verses like Romans 13:8 ("Owe no one anything," ESV). If that's your conviction, it's best not to violate your conscience (see Romans 14:23). But other verses encourage lending (Psalms 37:21, 26; 112:5), so an absolute prohibition may go too far. If we consider Romans 13 in its context, we read:

> Give to everyone what you owe them: If you owe taxes, pay taxes; if revenue, then revenue; if respect, then respect; if honor, then honor.
>
> Let no debt remain outstanding, except the continuing debt to love one another, for whoever loves others has fulfilled the law.
>
> *Romans 13:7–8*

The implication is, "Pay everyone what you owe them — taxes, revenue, respect, and honor. Pay your bills faithfully. If you take out a loan, make all your payments on time and in full. Honor your financial commitments. Display integrity."

Even if debt is permissible, it always involves a measure of risk because none of us know what our futures hold. How quickly you'll get a job, how much you'll be earning — these aren't things you can be certain about. Plus, once you factor in the interest, you'll have to pay back more than what you borrowed. Sometimes much more. So don't take out a loan except as a last resort, and only after you've considered the ramifications. If you make the choice to borrow, at least go in with your eyes wide open.

A Word to Nonreligious Readers

The Bible informs my perspective on the value of responsibility, hard work, personal integrity, and the dangers of debt. But although I'm writing as a Christian, this isn't a densely religious book. The topics discussed — why college is expensive, how to pay for it, how to earn more money as a student, how to set yourself up for success — are issues that affect you regardless of whether or not you share my religious beliefs.

Some people distinguish between "bad debt" and "good debt." Racking up credit card bills by staying at a five-star hotel in Hawaii for a month is considered bad debt. You didn't *need* a monthlong vacation, and it's not as if it got you something that can rise in value over time, like a house. By the same logic, student loan debt is considered to be good because college graduates generally earn more than noncollege graduates over the course of a lifetime. That's true in general, but this approach is too simplistic, for several reasons:

1. Once you start taking out student loans because, "Hey, I don't want to end up flipping burgers for the rest of my life," there's no telling how much debt you'll accumulate. Why? Because it's easier to spend Other People's Money (Uncle Sam's and the bank's, in this case) than it is to part with our own. While writing this chapter, I've been chatting with a few former students on Facebook. They all say the same thing: "I had no idea how much debt I was generating until I got out of school!" But there's no reason not to keep track of this number (see Trap 5). And actually, it's possible to get a decent education *without* taking on a mountain of debt. I'll show you how (see Trap 3).

2. Forty-four percent of people who pursue a four-year college degree don't graduate in six years, if ever.[7] Read that sentence again, slowly. If you're not academically motivated, have barely graduated from high school, and were only accepted to college because your heart was beating, you're considered a "high retention risk" in the

higher education world. Don't fall for the lie that a traditional four-year college experience is right for everyone. In Trap 1, I'll give you some other options. There are plenty of honorable, high-paying professions that are best pursued with alternative (and less expensive) forms of training, such as getting an associate degree, going to a trade school, or doing an apprenticeship.

3. Many students today change their majors at least once and as a result take more than four years to graduate. An extra year or two of college adds to their total price tag. Consider that tuition, room, and board all get more expensive every year. In Traps 3 and 4, I'll offer a few ideas to help you graduate faster.

4. You can't cash out your college education to pay off your loans. Think about it. If you finance a house but after a while life happens and you can't afford the payments, you can at least sell the house and recover whatever a buyer is willing to pay for it. But you can't sell back your college degree, even if you paid $100,000 for it. No one can buy that cool English Lit class you took. At best, you can sell back your books—at a loss.

Used College Education—50 Percent Off!

Craigslist Ad

Chance of a lifetime! This degree cost me $100,000, but I'm selling it for only $50,000! My loss is your gain. The $50K gets you every class I took. Contact me soon, and we'll work something out on my old books too.

e-mail: RegretfulStudent@sadlife.com

5. If at some point you can't make your student loan payments, you have little to no bankruptcy protection. Your lenders can come after you for the money you borrowed, the interest accrued, and even the cost to find you. If you have a job, they can garnish your wages. If you have a tax refund, they can grab that. Your credit rating will be

trashed. And if you're still in debt when it comes time to collect on your Social Security benefits (assuming there's anything left by then), the feds can snatch some of that too. They can chase you to the grave.

I don't mean to scare you, but we live in a culture that has grown dangerously comfortable with borrowing money. As of May 2011, Americans owed $2.43 trillion and saved a piddly 1.2 percent of their income. There were more than one million bankruptcy filings in 2013.[8] Younger adults (ages twenty-five to thirty-four) have the second highest rate of bankruptcy, right behind thirty-five to forty-four-year-olds. One out of four adults admits to not paying his or her bills on time. And nearly one in five Americans aged eighteen to twenty-four considers himself or herself to be in "debt hardship."[9]

Think about the totality of your life *before* taking out student loans. Aside from limiting the pursuit of your dreams, as well as the stress that debt tends to cause, bringing a high debt load into a marriage can lead to arguments about money, which are a top trigger for divorce. If you would like to qualify for a home mortgage someday or start a family and maybe work part-time or stay home with your kids, think about how debt might interfere.

The Cost of College Is Confusing

We all know college used to be much cheaper. But the problem is not just that college is expensive. It's that the process of figuring out what it's going to cost is beyond confusing. You never know what a college is actually going to cost *you* until after you've applied and received a financial aid offer. It all depends on the grants, scholarships, and tuition discounts you get for singing in the choir, playing on the tennis team, maintaining a certain GPA, or whatever.

You can better estimate your expenses and total debt load through graduation once you know what it will cost for that first year. But I'm going to show you a few websites that will help you *predict in advance* how much financial aid a college *should* give you, based on what they've given in the past to students like you.

And apart from the financial aid craziness, the cost of your college education will depend on what you decide is essential to the experience.

The Essential and the Peripheral

When I went to college, the food was terrible and the beds were hard. We joked about it and complained about it, but mainly we just dealt with it. It wasn't why we were there. Today? Competing for students has become bigger business, which is why you're getting more advertisements from colleges than I ever got, which was way more than what your parents got. (Don't worry. The marketing expense for those glossy brochures and professionally produced DVDs has been added to your tuition.)

How do colleges try to win your heart? One way is to have state-of-the-art amenities. Not just up-to-date classrooms, laboratories, libraries, and academic resources — though they certainly help and actually matter. We're talking gourmet food, sushi bars, rock-climbing walls, first-class fitness centers, and classy apartment-style housing. Don't have time to wash your clothes? Some colleges even boast a laundry and dry-cleaning service to help with that. Of course, these niceties make the college experience more enjoyable. But someone *is* paying for it, and it's either the government, rich donors, or you (hint: look at the "fees" line on your bill).

Considering the price of college, and your budget, be realistic about what's essential and what's peripheral. I've known students who were horrified at the thought of moving home with their parents and commuting to campus in order to save money. But think about it: Emily would have avoided debt entirely by living with her Uncle Chris and Aunt Jennifer. Living on campus is great, but room and board can run more than twice what it would cost to live with relatives, which *is* — believe it or not — what most students do.[10] You'll have to pay back every penny, plus all the interest, when you graduate. And if you're covering both tuition *and* living costs with loans, you're probably maxing out on federal loans and diving into private loans. Private loans have higher interest rates, which translates into higher monthly payments after you graduate — and your bill can go up from one month to another because the interest rates are often variable. For these and other reasons we'll discuss, it's best to avoid private loans entirely.

It Will Take Commitment

Going to college without racking up a huge bill is not easy. It'll require you to take some bold steps that go against the flow. Not going broke is about paying for things with cash whenever possible and minimizing expenses. It'll require *delaying gratification* — saying no to something good today so you can say yes to something better tomorrow, such as being free to pursue your dreams after graduation.

What is so dangerous about debt is that it promotes *instant gratification*. You can have it now! But think about it. Why is it so easy to borrow money — either by credit card or by student loans? Because the folks lending you the money are making a handsome profit on you. Sometimes it works out. Students graduate, move into high-paying jobs, and pay off their debts without major difficulty; others aren't so fortunate.

I am convinced there *is* a better way. Stay with me, because what I have to say in this book may surprise you. It will definitely empower you. You don't have to take on a mountain of debt just to have a shot at a decent future. You *can* go to college without mortgaging your future. Plenty of people are doing it, even today, and you can join them.

PART 1

EXAMINING ASSUMPTIONS
THINKING REALISTICALLY

EVERYONE MUST GO TO A FOUR-YEAR COLLEGE

Be true to how you're wired

Many people saunter into a four-year college with far less critical thought than they give to the decision to buy a car. I'm not talking about the question of *which* four-year college to attend; I'm talking about the decision to go in the first place. Too often, it's more of an assumption than a decision.

This chapter is about examining that assumption. Like a snowboard, an iPad, a car, or any other major purchase, a four-year college education is a product. It's something you purchase—with lots of money. Unlike other products, it also costs you lots of time. It's dangerous to assume it's necessary to buy something, especially if that something comes with a hefty price tag. It's smart to consider if our desires fall under the umbrella of "needs" or "wants." And no matter what you may have heard, four-year colleges are not for everyone. They're especially not for everyone who's barely eighteen and has just finished high school.

Perhaps you've never asked yourself whether or not you should go to a four-year college. Maybe you think, *Of course I'm going to college! High school is wrapping up soon. What else would I do next?* Rest assured, you haven't picked up an anti-college screed. I'm assuming that anyone reading this book is either hoping to get a degree or is in the process of getting one. And for good reason. Just about all of us need some kind of degree, certification, or advanced training to be successful in the twenty-first century workforce.

But that doesn't mean everyone should pursue a bachelor's

degree immediately after high school. What kind of training to get, when to get it, and where to get it are decisions you should make in a deliberate manner. If what you're after is a ticket to the middle class, a bachelor's degree is not the only way to get there, and depending on how you're wired, it may not be the best way. Let me at least give you several equally valid, less expensive, and less time-consuming alternatives to consider.

A four-year college is too expensive to wander into just because it's somehow expected of you or because you have nothing better to do. *Only go to a four-year college if it makes sense.*

Three Reasons to Reconsider the "Go Right to a Four-Year College" Assumption

1. Getting accepted into a four-year college may not mean much. That probably sounds weird or even rude, so let me explain. Throughout most of U.S. history, getting accepted into a four-year college was itself a big deal. It meant you had done well in your previous schooling and that your teachers along with the college admissions folks recognized your potential for greater intellectual feats. College was for the few, not the many. But it's not like those who didn't go to college were condemned to a life of poverty. They went on to enjoy meaningful jobs, stable careers, and middle-class lifestyles. As recently as 1970, only one in four members of the middle-class workforce had *any* formal education beyond high school.[1]

But then low-skill jobs started disappearing, and college graduates began to see their earnings rise dramatically, particularly those in fields like technology, finance, law, and health care. High schools and parents got the memo and ramped up a campaign to pitchfork more teens into the halls of higher education. By 1990, about six in ten high school graduates immediately headed to college, and by the year 2002, that figure had reached 65 to 70 percent, where it remains today.[2]

As the number of students going to college was rapidly increasing, the number of colleges was also on the rise.[3] You may recognize the terms *supply* and *demand*. When there is a lot of demand for

a product—higher education, in this case—it invites more participants to enter the market. More than one out of three of today's four-
year colleges did not exist in 1980. As these new colleges popped
up, many of them implemented an open admissions policy, a trend
that had begun a decade or two earlier. As long as an applicant met
certain minimum standards (test scores, high school GPA)—and in
some cases, no standard other than a GED or high school diploma—
they were guaranteed admission.[4]

Now where did this open admission trend come from? On the
one hand, there was a sincere desire to give everyone a crack at a college education. To the extent that a slew of high-paying careers were
increasingly accessible only to those with a bachelor's degree, colleges viewed minimal entrance standards as a means of avoiding elit-
ism. The value of everyone having equal access to all that America
represents had gripped the nation in the days of Martin Luther King
Jr. and the Civil Rights movement. Colleges were simply following
suit. If someone had completed high school and aspired to earn a
bachelor's degree, why would you deny him or her that opportunity?

But there's also a more cynical interpretation: The colleges
wanted the extra business. Tuition dollars are the lifeblood of all
but the most elite colleges and universities. New colleges in particular often feel compelled to attract more students in order to pay
their bills, service their debt, and develop their limited and often
dilapidated infrastructure. In 2013, education expert Jeffrey Selingo
estimated that one-third of all colleges were on an unsustainable
financial path, and another quarter of colleges were in serious risk of
joining them.[5] And a 2014 survey of college and university presidents
found that only half were confident in their institution's financial
model over the next decade.[6]

Colleges that are desperate for tuition dollars are more than
happy to squeeze a few more students into a classroom. The upshot
is that if you graduate from high school and have a pulse, you can
probably get into college *somewhere*.[7] Frank Brock, a former president
of Covenant College (a respected Christian college in Georgia), put
it this way: "Students used to worry about getting into college; today
enrollment-driven colleges worry about getting students."[8] That's

why you probably have a large box of college advertisement mail and why you see ads and billboards for colleges everywhere, especially niche graduate programs in fields you didn't know existed.

Maybe you'd be the first member of your family to graduate from a four-year college. Everyone is pushing you to just waltz into the financial aid office, secure a slew of loans, and get on with it. But just because a college wants you doesn't mean you should want them. And just because a college wants you doesn't mean you'll graduate, which leads me to the next point.

2. Almost half (44 percent) of those who start off at four-year colleges or universities haven't graduated … six years later.[9] Almost no one starts college thinking he or she is going to be in that statistic, yet that's where almost half of incoming freshmen end up. Graduation rates are much higher at some colleges than others, but high school academic performance and a student's financial status are remarkably good predictors. So the good news is that you can size up your chances of making it right from the get-go. Of those who finished high school in the bottom 40 percent of their high school class, three out of four will not complete a bachelor's degree, even if given eight and a half years to do so.[10] Among incoming students told they need to repeat high school level coursework (a.k.a., be remediated), only one in three will complete his or her bachelor's degree in six years.[11] The upshot? If high school academics weren't your thing, a traditional four-year college probably won't be either.[12] Do something else.

Financial status is an even stronger predictor of college success than high school academic performance. *Regardless of academic ability*, it's reported that among students whose families are in the bottom income quartile (lowest 25 percent), only 8 percent will earn their bachelor's degree by age twenty-four. But if your family is in the top income quartile, your odds of having a bachelor's degree at age twenty-four are better than 80 percent.[13]

How much sense does that make? It's heartbreaking. Many of us grew up believing that social mobility—the idea that if you work hard and play by the rules, you can begin life in poverty but rise as high as your talents, efforts, and accomplishments take you—is the birthright for all Americans. But we're not seeing enough of it these days. Good people of various persuasions are debating how to increase social mobility and college graduation rates, but since this isn't a public policy book, I'm not planning to go there. I want to focus on how *you* can beat the college debt trap. Today. Regardless of our broken system. Because if there's one thing I've learned, it's

FACTOID

The United States has the highest college dropout rate in the industrialized world. While seven out of ten high school graduates go on to college, less than half of twenty-five- to thirty-four-year-olds (44 percent) have a college degree of any sort.[14]

that you can't wait until the world is perfect to start doing what only you can do to build a better life.

We'll talk later about how to lower the expense of college. For now, let's just observe that it's important to count the cost before even starting. Make sure you have what it takes to graduate — financially, academically, and in terms of personal commitment and discipline. A four-year college or university can be a great investment, but you really do need to graduate.

Caveat: Regardless of your family income, if you were a top student in high school, or you did well on your SAT or ACT, do not assume that four-year colleges will be too pricey. There are schools out there with the resources to be generous to students like you. More about this in Trap 3.

3. Attending a four-year college is superexpensive. This isn't a reason *never* to pursue a bachelor's degree. It's perhaps a reason to delay that pursuit until you've earned or saved enough money to at least start college relatively debt-free. And if your parents are planning on helping you pay for college, they could use the extra time as well. Avoiding loans, especially in the early years, is a great strategy, because the less time interest is accruing, the less you end up having to pay back.[15]

Even if you go for a bachelor's degree, there are expensive ways and inexpensive ways to earn one (as we'll discuss in Trap 3). The former can lock you into years of crushing debt, as it did for my friend Michael. He spent five years at a community college followed by four years at a university until he finally picked up his bachelor's degree—and more than $80,000 of debt. Some ten months after graduating, he landed a job with the county as an environmental safety inspector. He's now thirty and living with his parents, who are helping him pay off his loans and avoid bankruptcy.

So if a four-year college isn't the best move for you, or at least not the best move right away, what else is out there? Let me walk you through a few alternatives, all of which can save you tens of thousands of dollars now, and none of which close the door on getting your bachelor's degree later.

Alternatives to Going Straight from High School to a Four-Year College

1. Get an associate's degree in a strategic, marketable field. In 2014, of the 18 million students in undergraduate programs, 7.3 million were at two-year colleges.[16] That's not terribly lopsided, but many of those two-year students don't ultimately earn associate degrees.[17] They just pick up credits on the cheap and, if all goes well, transfer them into bachelor's degree programs—usually a smart, cost-saving move.

There's nothing wrong with wanting a bachelor's degree. It's what I did, and it worked out great. But here's the thing: Depending on what field you pursue, there may or may not be a job waiting on the other side. A 2010 report from Georgetown University economists predicted that future job openings for college graduates will be split roughly fifty-fifty between those requiring bachelor's or advanced degrees and those requiring associate's degrees or occupational certificates.[18] But in 2012, bachelor's degree recipients outstripped associate's degree recipients by about 75 percent.[19]

Part of the problem is that many high school guidance counselors, teachers, and parents look down on associate's degrees as second class, mere consolation prizes for those who can't cut it at "real" colleges, and one-way tickets to a lower income and a less fulfilling life. So they push everyone to the four-year colleges and universities, which, as I explained earlier, virtually any high school graduate can get into these days.

But are these negative perceptions about associate's degrees accurate? The graph below shows the annual salaries for three occupations that you can access with an associate's degree, each of which the Bureau of Labor Statistics expects to be among the fastest-growing fields through 2020.[20] The average salary for someone with a bachelor's degree is also shown for comparison.[21]

Average Annual Salary — 2012

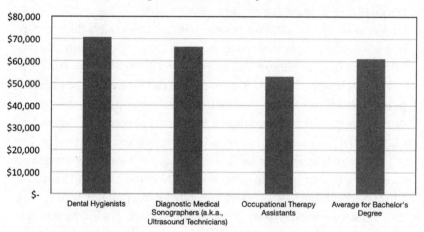

It turns out you can do well with an associate's degree compared to a bachelor's degree, especially considering that an associate's degree can usually be earned in less time and at less cost.

FACTOID

Economists predict almost as many job openings for associate's degrees and occupational certificates as for bachelor's and advanced degrees. About 28 percent of workers with associate's degrees earn more than the median earnings of workers with bachelor's degrees.[22]

A handful of states have begun publishing the average earnings of recent graduates from two-year and four-year colleges for the spectrum of disciplines that students can pursue.[23] Texas found that "a year after graduation, students with two-year technical degrees have first-year median earnings of more than $50,000, just over $11,000 more than graduates of bachelor's degree programs across the state." In Colorado, one year after graduation, students with career-oriented Associate of Applied Sciences (AAS) degrees were "earning almost $7,000 more than graduates of bachelor's degree programs across the state." In Virginia, "graduates of occupational/technical associate's degree programs, with an average salary of just under $40,000, out-earned not only nonoccupational associate's degree graduates—by about $6,000—but also bachelor's degree graduates by almost $2,500 statewide."[24] You get the picture.

Keep in mind that *most* people with an associate's degree earn less than *most* people with a bachelor's degree.[25] So to earn a higher salary, you have to choose a strategic field (the health care and technology sectors are strong). Also note that the figures in the previous paragraph are for *recent* graduates. Over the long run, bachelor's degree recipients can experience large salary increases, depending on their industry and especially if they move into management. But it's also true that an associate's degree can be a stepping-stone to a bachelor's degree or some other advanced certificate. In the meantime, you're out of school faster and earning real money sooner.

2. Learn a skilled trade. While many college graduates struggle to find full-time work in their field, on the other side of the spectrum, we've got employers complaining that they can't find enough people with the right skills to hire. Manpower Group, a North American–based multinational human resource consulting firm, conducts a massive annual survey to identify which jobs employers have the most difficulty filling. At the top of the list, for four years in a row (2010–2013), are skilled trade workers.[26] Think electricians, welders, mechanics, HVACR technicians, and so on.

Why don't we have enough skilled trade workers? Here's how Manpower put it in their 2012 Talent Shortage Survey report: "As educational systems around the world have focused on four-year university education, this has resulted in the decline of vocational/technical programs—both curricula and enrollments have eroded over the past several decades. In addition, with fewer new workers to offset current retirements in the skilled trades, many economies will face continued shortages in the future."[27]

What they're saying is that the "everyone should go to a four-year college" pendulum has swung too far. Many high schools have emphasized four-year college preparation at the expense of vocational preparation. High school classes such as auto repair, welding, electronics, and woodworking have largely gone the way of the dinosaur. I think Advanced Placement and International Baccalaureate classes are important, but there needs to be a balance. We all depend on skilled workers to provide us with paved roads, indoor plumbing, new buildings, working electricity, and much more. While our economy needs more well-trained four-year college graduates, we also need more young adults with strategic associate's degrees or certificates in the skilled trades.[28] With only 44 percent of the twenty-five- to thirty-four-year-old population having any sort of post-high school degree, we must have an "all of the above" approach.

The other factor is that skilled trade workers are retiring faster than we're replacing them. Employees tend to be older (53 percent are over forty-five), but they're also more likely to hang it up at sixty-five.[29] That bodes well for those at the beginning of their careers. Work hard, and your skills, income, and opportunities should grow.

Age	Percent of skilled trade workers in the U.S.	Overall U.S. workforce
45–older	53 percent	44 percent
55–64	19 percent	16 percent
65–older	2 percent	5 percent

So how do you get started in the skilled trades? Either at a trade school (a.k.a. vocational school) or through a registered apprenticeship. Both combine classroom instruction with hands-on training, and with either, check them out thoroughly before enrolling. Some trade schools are affordable, accredited with the appropriate agency, and boast high graduation rates, top-notch instructors, and a stellar job placement record. It's best if they grant an associate's degree (such as an Associate of Applied Sciences) at the completion of their training. Others are expensive, unaccredited, and have low graduation and job placement rates. Not surprisingly, these schools have higher student loan default rates.

Apprenticeships range from one to six years, averaging about four years. Most of the time apprentices earn while they learn. You'd want to choose from one of the twenty-one thousand or so registered programs throughout the country. The Office of Apprenticeship (OA) works in conjunction with independent State Apprenticeship Agencies (SAAs) to monitor the quality of these programs and to ensure the safety of some 350,000 participants.[30] Their website is www.doleta.gov/oa.

3. Join the military. Enlisting in the armed services is a brave and big commitment. The military's primary task is to defend the U.S.'s national security interests at home and abroad (as determined by fallible political leaders). But if you have the physical and emotional fortitude to participate, it's an honorable profession that will equip you for adulthood in profound ways. The military offers exceptional on-the-job training and provides generous educational funding for traditional colleges. You can either be a full-time student while in the military (for example, through an ROTC program), or you can go to college full-time after you leave the service. Either way, it's all on Uncle Sam's dime, including books and living expenses, assuming you put in the required time of service. The veterans I've had as college students have always been characterized by maturity, a strong work ethic, and a deep sense of personal responsibility. And if you serve for ten years, even after you've completed college or dropped out along the way, the government will forgive all your federal student loans.

Jacob's Story

I joined the Navy because after sitting at a desk for twelve years, four years of college seemed like an eternity. Two recruiters convinced me that the educational opportunities in the Navy were abundant. I signed up for their Nuclear Propulsion Program. It offered training that was sure to make me a success, whether I stayed in the military for twenty years or got out as soon as my mandatory service was completed. Little did I know that the Navy would send me to several different training commands (schools by a different name) and that I wouldn't report to my first ship until sixteen months after I had joined. While I was in the service the Navy paid for my associate's degree via the Tuition Assistance Program. I ended up getting out after six years and getting a job as an operations technician at an air separation plant. One of the reasons I was hired was my military service and the training I received in the Navy. Later I used the GI Bill and went back to college, graduating with a BS degree in Nuclear Engineering.

4. Take a year off before college. Earlier I mentioned the advantage of delaying college to give you and maybe your parents a chance to put away some money. That requires you having a job that pays enough to let you save for college—a greater likelihood if you've got an associate's degree, trade school certification, or a marketable skill (maybe photography, website design, or teaching piano). But apart from the possibility of saving money, if you're almost done with high school and aren't sure what you want to do next, consider taking a year off.

Here's why. Changing majors is a big reason that the *majority* of students take more than four years to complete their bachelor's degree, which usually means taking on more debt. But a year off between high school and college can help you get a better sense of who you are and what you want to study. If you go this route, I recommend keeping yourself busy with structured, intentional pursuits.[31] The last thing you want to do is waste thirty hours per week playing video games and chatting on social media. Clocking twenty to thirty hours per week in a good part-time job, taking classes in an area of interest at a local community college, shadowing a professional who works in a field you're considering, studying to improve your ACT/ SAT test scores, and learning more about different college majors, including associate's degrees and skilled trades, are all legitimate ways to spend the time. In other words, use this year to become more focused on specific professional objectives; on developing personal discipline, study skills, and a work ethic; and on getting a better idea of the kind of academic or technical training you'll need to achieve your professional aspirations. You'll be more likely to make a straight path through college, which will save you a ton of money.

If you're a high achiever, there's something to be said for getting off the performance treadmill for a year and pursuing a structured service or entrepreneurial experience, such as doing missions work, serving with AmeriCorps, carrying out community or church-related service, getting a cross-cultural experience, or starting a business. Many find it to be a transformative experience, one that expands their horizons and gives them a wider outlook on life and what they hope to become. They return to the academic world invigorated and with a greater sense of purpose and focus. And if what you do in this "gap year" is somehow connected to your professional aspirations, you'll have a taste of what's waiting for you on the other side of school.[32] That sense of informed anticipation will motivate you to do well.

Caveat: Watch your budget. You don't want to go broke *before* you go to college.

The Bottom Line

Are you ready for college? Here are a few questions to help you assess if you're ready to take on the financial and academic commitment of a traditional four-year college:

1. How well did you do in high school? If you did poorly, or if high school was a long time ago, it's best to ease into the college workload. Take one or two classes per semester at a community college or through an inexpensive online program — classes that are sure to count toward a four-year degree. If you have a high-paying day job, keep it while earning credits on the side. But work with the college's advising office to make sure you're taking classes that will count toward your bachelor's degree.

2. Are you emotionally ready to sit in a chair and study for forty hours per week for the next four to five years? If you'd rather do something that combines thinking and doing, consider a skilled trade or an associate's degree. You don't have to jump through the academic hoops and be like everyone else. Skilled tradespeople will always be in demand. And mechanics, electricians, and dental hygienists can never have their jobs shipped overseas.

3. If you've decided college is for you, and you're emotionally ready to go, what can you afford, not just now, but for the next five years, assuming tuition goes up, say, 5 percent per year? Also factor in living costs, including books. (More on this in Trap 3.)

4. How well do you know what you want to major in? The better you know your strengths and interests, and the careers they can lead to, the less likely you are to change majors. (More on this in Trap 4.)

But before we talk about choosing a college and a major, we need to examine our assumptions about paying for college and who's responsible when we sign that oh-so-convenient loan paperwork. That's what we'll tackle in Trap 2.

TRAP 2

IT'S ALL JUST GOING TO WORK OUT

Understand why college is expensive and take responsibility for how you pay for it

"We did what we were told to do: go to college, get an education, you'll get a job, you'll get a house, you'll be cool," Rose Swidden said. Rose was about to graduate from the State University of New York (SUNY) Cobleskill with a degree in agriculture—and $35,000 in student loan debt. "And that's what we did. And now here we are done with it—and now what?"[1]

Jessica stepped forward: "I did everything I was supposed to do. I went to college and graduated. Now I'm a waitress with a master's degree, barely scraping by."

And Matthew: "I'm twenty-four years old and am $90,000 in debt from getting a college education. Why are we punished for getting a higher education? College was supposed to make my life easier, but now I can barely make my loan payments."[2]

It was the fall of 2011 and the heyday of the Occupy Wall Street protests. Students, graduates, and dropouts all across the country were decrying the burden of student loan debt. There was a palpable sense of helplessness and indignation. Some were demanding the immediate forgiveness of their student loan debt, insisting they got a raw deal.

Now travel with me to just about any campus in America. Let's walk up to a few random students and ask them about their loans.

Based on experience, I expect a lot of conversations will sound like this:

> "May we ask you about student loans?
>
> "Yeah, I've got a couple of loans."
>
> "Do you know how much you'll owe when you graduate?"
>
> "Not really. It's complicated. Each of the loans works differently."
>
> "Do you know how much your monthly payments will be when you graduate?"
>
> "No, but I'm sure it's all going to work out somehow."

As they say, ignorance is bliss. But it doesn't take long for naive optimism to morph into the disillusionment we saw in Rose, Jessica, and Matthew. The dream of a college degree can quickly become a student loan nightmare.

I want you to avoid that fate. (Too late for that? Keep reading. We'll talk later about getting free.) In this chapter, we'll take a hard look at the assumption that "everything will work out," no matter how much money you borrow for college and what kind of job you get when you graduate. While that may be how things *should* work in a perfect world, you owe it to yourself to understand how things *actually* work in the real world.

Why Is College So Expensive?

The price of college has risen faster than the rate of inflation for more than thirty years. Even when people's salaries aren't rising or when the economy is slumping, the price of college always finds a way to go up. How?

I remember the first time I paid more than ten bucks to see a movie in a theater. I looked at my friend and said, "How can they charge that much?" He quipped, "We just paid them. That's how." Simple enough. Theaters are able to charge that much because we are willing to pay. People like to see movies. There are only so many theaters in town. They all charge about the same price because they can.

It makes sense. When business is slow, restaurants and stores lower their prices or announce specials. When business is booming, the discounts go away, as the folks are willing to pay full freight. The comparison isn't perfect, but it's unquestionable that demand for higher education has grown tremendously during the last few decades. From 1980 to 2010, colleges saw an 80 percent increase in enrollment while the price of college skyrocketed.[3] When lots of people want something, it tends to cost more.

Why are we willing to pay through the nose for something that we complain is too expensive? Because we view college as essential for accessing high-salary lines of work, avoiding unemployment, and obtaining intangible social benefits. And because, if needed, we can borrow the necessary funds, regardless of our financial status or prospects.

The perception that a college degree helps a person earn more money is generally accurate. If you have a bachelor's degree, you'll probably earn much more than someone with only a high school degree (and usually more than someone with an associate's degree — though not always, especially in the early years, as we explained in the last chapter). It depends on your major and what industry you go into, but the so-called "earnings premium" of a bachelor's degree has been rising over time.[4]

And yes, if you've got a bachelor's degree, it gives you a leg up when it comes to finding just about any kind of job.[5] Apart from how much you learned, your degree serves as a signal to employers, telling them you had the perseverance to show up, be faithful, and knock out about 120 units of post–high school level coursework. If given the choice between a college graduate and a noncollege graduate, most employers will go with the one who has the sheepskin.

What's been the response to all this demand for college? New colleges have been created, and many existing schools have expanded their infrastructure to accommodate more students. They are spending lots of money on new construction — academic buildings, libraries, laboratories, and so on — and hiring more highly trained professors along with more administrative staff and support personnel. When I went to college, the Internet was just becoming popular.

Campuses were busy wiring all their buildings. But less than ten years later, they were forced to add *wireless* Internet access, first in their academic spaces and soon everywhere else. Today with the proliferation of laptops, cell phones, and tablets, all competing for Internet access, even small colleges have spent millions of dollars upgrading their network's bandwidth while adding new levels of security to ward off viruses, hackers, and so on. Information technology infrastructure has dramatically increased the cost of new academic buildings. Similarly, the need for the latest and greatest equipment has escalated the cost of new science, engineering, and other laboratory-intensive buildings. Someone's got to pay for all this.

But there's another benefit we assign to college, and this one is more intangible than professional. I'm talking about the social aspect — the desire to make new friends, create precious memories, and just have a good time. These are things most of us want from college, even if we can't measure their value in dollars and cents. While relationships and camaraderie have always been a part of the college experience, the expense associated with providing students the "appropriate ambiance" has drastically increased. When I went to college, the food was mediocre at best, and the choices were few. We joked about it and complained about it, but mainly we just dealt with it. It wasn't why we were there. The dining halls of today are much ... swankier. Beyond the classy architecture, they offer a wider variety of higher-quality food than I ever saw (gourmet options, sushi bars, Mongolian BBQ, and other fine delicacies).

Traditional dorms, like the one I lived in — think small, cinderblock, two-person cells with bunk beds, community bathrooms and showers, and a bare-bones lounge with out-of-style, second-rate furniture, and a low-quality TV — are increasingly rare. Since 1995, fewer than one in five new residence halls have been of this sort.[6] The majority are now apartment-style suites — "living and learning centers" equipped with spacious, lavishly furnished lobbies, game

> **When I went to college, the food was mediocre at best, and the choices were few. We joked about it and complained about it, but mainly we just dealt with it. It wasn't why we were there.**

rooms, flat-screen TVs, well-lit study rooms, and, in some cases, fitness centers, ATMs, and convenience stores all built in. Recreation centers equipped with rock climbing walls and hot tubs are also on the rise, as are state-of-the-art student centers. The cost per bed in student housing has risen by about 75 percent in the last ten years.[7] Those who have observed the shift say living on some campuses is more like living in a hotel than a dorm.

What's driving this trend for plush accommodations? Rising enrollment has led to more competition between colleges for prospective students. There are many more colleges and universities to choose from today than there were a few decades ago. Schools are looking for ways to stand out in a crowded field. They're hoping a beautiful campus with top-dollar amenities will get your attention the same way a clean, well-staged, updated home with excellent curb appeal attracts more buyers. And guess what? It works. So colleges mimic and compete with each other, leading to a splurge in collective spending.

There's a noncollege factor that ties into all this: Living space per person in the United States has doubled over the last forty years.[8] That means a growing number of you probably aren't thrilled at the idea of community bathrooms. Sharing personal space with a total stranger is intrusive and uncool. Colleges are tapping into the desires of their "customers," outdoing one another in what critics call "an amenities arms race."

At least two other factors have contributed to the rising cost of college. One, *state funding for public universities has been down over the last decade.* States have in essence told their colleges to make students pay more so the states can contribute less. That's obviously a tougher pill to swallow for lower-income students. Two, *schools are becoming more bureaucratic.* Over the last twenty years, colleges have been hiring administrators at twice the rate of faculty.[9] There's been a growth in the number of highly paid assistant vice presidents and deans with complicated job titles. This has been particularly true of large public university systems, some of which, even in the face of steep budget cuts, were decreasing course offerings rather than axing unessential personnel.[10]

All of these factors have contributed to the price of college rising faster than the price of other goods and services. Family incomes certainly aren't keeping up, so where do students come up with the money? Three other sources are picking up the slack.[11] One, *colleges are giving out more cash* in the form of scholarships (dipping into their endowments or raising additional funds from donors). They're trying to sweeten the deal to get new students to commit, especially if you have a higher SAT/ACT score or better grades than other applicants, or if you're a talented athlete or musician. Two, *state and federal grants have increased*, though not as much as some would prefer.[12] And three, *student loans are on the rise*. Ah, yes. In the class of 1993, only 45 percent of students borrowed a dime for college, including from family members.[13] Fast-forward twenty years to the class of 2013, and more than 70 percent borrowed money. The average debt load at graduation more than tripled in this time period.[14] That means more students maxing out on federal loans and dipping into private loans, which have higher interest rates and don't qualify for a host of loan forgiveness programs.

The easier it is for students to take out greater amounts of debt, the *faster* the price of college seems to rise.[15] The inescapable conclusion is that the proliferation of student loans is not, on the whole, making college more affordable. Let's take a closer look at this vicious cycle.

How Student Loans Make You Less Cost Conscious

Whenever you borrow money to pay for something, it makes you less sensitive to the price, since the money isn't coming out of your wallet, at least not today. Let's say you work hard and save $1,000 to buy a new laptop computer and a few other things for school. Whatever you don't spend on these items is yours to spend with your friends. You're probably going to shop around for the best value, because that $1,000 didn't fall from the sky. You worked for it, so you don't want to blow it. Now let's say your friend Samantha doesn't have a job, so I loan her $1,000. I tell her she can pay me back in four or five years, after she graduates and gets on her feet. When she goes out to spend that money on a laptop computer, tablet, or whatever, do you think she'll be as careful as you were?

If Samantha is like most people, the answer is no. A loan feels like a gift, especially if you don't need to even start paying it back for several years. It's easier to spend other people's money than it is to spend our own. So when the *majority* of people are spending other people's money to attend college, that means the majority of people are less sensitive to price — which means they're willing to pay higher prices.

> **When the *majority* of people are spending other people's money to attend college, that means the majority of people are less sensitive to price — which means they're willing to pay higher prices.**

The fact that it's easy for you to borrow money lowers the pressure on you to consider less expensive ways to get your degree. It also lowers the pressure on colleges to keep their costs under control, since students aren't *directly* feeling the pinch. So not only do colleges have a product you desperately want; you and your friends can and will borrow as much money as you need to pay for it. These conditions promote the opposite of cost consciousness.

What's a Subsidy?

The dictionary defines a subsidy as "money that is paid usually by a government to keep the price of a product or service low or to help a business or organization to continue to function." When the federal government makes loans available at below-market interest rates, this is a form of subsidization, since it allows people to borrow money on better terms than they otherwise could.

But when the federal student loan program uses the term *subsidized*, they're using it a bit differently.

On a *subsidized* federal student loan, the government pays the interest while you're in school at least *half-time. On an unsubsidized federal student loan, you must pay the interest (or let the loan principal snowball), even while you're in school.*

Nevertheless, as I write, the interest rate on an unsubsidized Federal Stafford Loan is only 4.66 percent for undergraduate students — far less than what would be offered by private lenders. So even here the concept of a subsidy is at work. You're getting money on better terms than you otherwise could.

When the price of college is subsidized, the bar is lowered, so more people "consume" the product. But as college enrollment rises, so does the price tag because higher demand leads to higher prices, especially since people demand quality, which means better facilities, more resources, and fancier amenities. Yet all that does is lead to more dependence on the subsidies, greater consumption, and even higher prices over time.

For evidence of the power of lending programs to desensitize us to how much we're paying, look no further than the popularity of payment plans with auto dealers. I remember buying my 2008 Toyota Sienna under a four-year, no-interest payment plan. The price of the minivan was divided by the number of months; it came to about $600 per month. During the last six months of my payment plan, I started to get mail from the good folks at Toyota. Did I want to trade in my "old" Sienna for a new, fancier minivan? They'd be happy to "discuss financing." My "payment would not increase." Did they think I was too dumb to understand that if I kept my Sienna, my payments were about to *decrease to zero*? The dealer wanted to keep money flowing from me to them on a monthly basis. So they were suggesting that four years was long enough to drive a car that was built to last more like fifteen to twenty years. But I was ready to be done making the payments and was more than happy with my "old" car. Interestingly, when I bought the car, they refused to give me a lower price if I paid them all cash, up front. No doubt they've discovered that lending programs earn them more money over the long haul.

It's reasonable to pay a chunk of change for a college degree. An education is a wonderful thing. My concern is with students taking out massive amounts of debt and assuming it's all just going to magically work out. Getting loans for college is super-easy, which has led to more students graduating with a ball and chain around their feet. Lots of prices rise over time—car prices, home prices, gas prices, and health care prices. But *no* price in the U.S. economy has risen as fast as the price of college, because for nothing else can so much money be so easily borrowed. The fast-rising price of college leads to *more* students needing *bigger* loans to afford college. This can't go on forever. Something's got to give. The growing popularity of less expensive online education is an example of a response.

> **No price in the U.S. economy has risen as fast as the price of college, because for nothing else can so much money be so easily borrowed.**

The good news is that by becoming a savvier customer, you can contribute to the solution. *To beat the college debt trap, you need to understand that it's always easier to spend money that's borrowed than it is to spend your own.* When you don't feel the pain of having to fork out your own cash, you tend to spend more. So be careful, because you'll end up paying back a lot more than what you borrowed. Just because you *can* take out more student loans doesn't mean you *should*.

To complicate matters, borrowing for college is unlike borrowing for anything else. To appreciate the uniqueness of student loans—and their danger—we must first understand how borrowing *usually* works.

How Borrowing *Usually* Works

Let's say James has money to lend. He will lend you some, but only if you agree to pay him back with interest. Why charge interest? Because James wants to earn a living and feed his family—and if he runs a company, he needs to pay his employees. Moreover, if James doesn't loan you the money, he could invest it elsewhere and earn a profit, perhaps in rental properties, mutual funds, stocks, bonds, CDs, or a simple money market account. Furthermore, you present a measure of risk. If you don't pay James back, he'll have to chase you to recover whatever he can. That possibility has to be factored in. So the interest rate that James offers you is based on:

- his opportunities elsewhere, which he's forgoing to lend you the money
- what others are charging (if he doesn't match or beat others, you could go elsewhere for a loan)
- how long you plan to borrow the money (a higher interest rate if you want to pay it back with lower payments over a longer period of time)
- the level of risk you represent (more risk = a higher interest rate)

James will make you fill out a credit report. He wants to know what kind of a track record you have for paying back loans. That tells him something about how much risk you represent. Perhaps you've never borrowed money to purchase a house, car, or other large item, but if you have a credit card, you're technically borrowing money every time you make a purchase. So he'll want to know if you pay off your Visa or MasterCard balance every month. The less faithful you are in fulfilling your financial obligations, the more risk you represent.

Maybe you've never had a loan or a credit card. No problem. Do you pay your rent on time, or does your landlord have to hunt you down and hit you with late fees? Do you stay on top of your bank account, or do you bounce checks? James will also want to know how much money you make and how secure your paychecks are. If you've got a steady job with a contract, that's preferable. If you make money from odd jobs — some months are good, others are lean — that's less than ideal. James will compare the amount you want to borrow with the amount you regularly earn, as this too helps him assess how much risk you represent.

Depending on how much you want to borrow and what you're borrowing it for, James will probably charge you an origination fee and/or an underwriting fee. An origination fee covers his costs to get you the money and also covers some of his overhead. An underwriting fee covers the final analysis and approval of your loan, including verification that the information you've provided is factual.[16]

Another thing James might look for is collateral. Put bluntly, what do you have of value that he could go after if you refused to make payment? The more assets you own, the more likely a judge is to require you to somehow make payment.

In summary, James considers all of these factors and either makes you a loan offer or doesn't. Probably he does, because he stands to gain in the transaction. He can simply tailor the interest rate according to the level of risk you pose. By receiving back his money with interest, along with any late fees, James makes money by lending it.

As I explained in the introduction, I don't think taking on debt is always wrong. We have to weigh the wisdom of each situation on its own merits. We must consider whether the extra burden that debt will bring us *tomorrow* is worth whatever it is that debt allows us to do *today*. And as we see in the example of James, lenders are usually performing their own risk assessment, since any failure on our part will become a burden to them as well.

But borrowing for college is different.

How Borrowing Money for College Is Different

When you borrow for college, the lenders don't check you out thoroughly, the way James did in the example above. You simply fill out the Federal Application for Free Student Aid (FAFSA), and it spits out an Expected Family Contribution (EFC).[17] The college's sticker price (also known as total cost of attendance or COA) minus any scholarships or grants you receive is your *net tuition*. It's at least as high as your EFC, and usually higher. The financial aid office will present you with a mix of grants, scholarships, work-study funding, and loans—all of which they call aid, even though some of it never needs to be repaid (grants and scholarships), some of it needs to be earned (work-study), and some of it must be repaid with interest (loans). That's why it's more helpful to talk about net tuition. If a university's annual sticker price is $45,000 (including room, board, and fees), but they're only making you cough up, earn, or borrow $15,000 (net tuition), that's probably a good deal.[18]

If you need to borrow money, and most students do, the financial aid folks walk you through the process and tell you where to sign.

It's their job to make it easy, but keep in mind that they work for the college, not for you. I'm not suggesting they're bad people. I'm just saying their job is to help you get money and enroll, not to give you unbiased, personal advice like, "Wow, if you need to borrow *that* much for your first year, are you sure this is the right university for you?" In fact, some would say that if they gave such advice, they'd open themselves to discrimination charges.

Elizabeth's Story

I'm the first in my family to attend college. As part of the enrollment process, my university automatically routed incoming freshmen to the financial aid office right after we signed up for classes. When my name was called, I walked in and found a seat next to my adviser's desk, and off we went. She tapped a few computer keys and brought up my bill, and after learning I'd completed the FAFSA, signed me up for the maximum amount of federal loans. I was given a two-minute explanation on how those loans worked and was directed to also get a private loan, because the federal ones wouldn't cover everything.

When filling out the application for a private loan, I was surprised to discover a little box that let me type in the amount of money I wanted — like writing my own paycheck. Wow, I thought, that was too easy. I had just amassed close to $10,000 in debt — more than three times my life savings — and it was only the first semester! I'd repeat this experience several times in the next few years, knowing that my only hope of ever paying it off was to graduate and get a good job. I had no idea how much I owed until six months after graduation when it came time to start paying it all back.

By the way, when you borrow money for college, the school gets paid right away — and that money stays with the school, regardless of how difficult it becomes for you to pay it off years later. The college is not sharing in your financial risk, except insofar as it is obligated to track and report its student loan default rate. A high default rate could deter future students from enrolling. Worst case, it can cause a college to lose its access to federal grants and loans. Still, it's not like Uncle Sam or Wells Fargo is going to knock on Big U's door, looking for the money you owe. It's all on you, so it's your job to know what you're getting into.

When you apply for a federal student loan, no one does a credit check to see how much risk you represent.[19] There's no consideration as to whether you have any collateral with which to pay back the lender, which is odd because, unlike a car or home, a college education is intangible. No one can take back your education if you later refuse to pay for it.

If I wanted to borrow twenty million dollars to buy a large, upscale home overlooking the ocean, no bank on the planet would lend me that kind of money. They would ask me enough questions to find out that I could never afford the mortgage payments. So why would Uncle Sam allow you to borrow tens of thousands of dollars without some level of confidence that you'll have the means to pay the money back?

Here's why: The federal government has extraordinary power to collect what you owe them. If you have a job, it can garnish your wages. If you have a tax refund, Uncle Sam can grab that. The collection agency can trash your credit rating, making it difficult for you to find a job (since many employers check credit ratings). And if you're still in debt when you reach your golden years, the feds can raid your Social Security benefits (assuming there's anything left). You can't escape, even if you declare bankruptcy.

It gets crazier. If you're a French literature major at a third-rate college, your ability to borrow Uncle Sam's money for college is no different than if you're an electrical engineering major at a world-renowned university. Never mind that most French literature graduates make less money and are more likely to be underemployed than electrical engineering graduates from top schools. *Private* lenders might consider your major and earning prospects in determining your interest rate, but the federal government won't.

The upshot is that just about any would-be college student can walk into the financial aid office of any university and borrow as much money as he or she needs to fund whatever educational pursuits his or her heart desires, all the way through to the PhD level. So don't comfort yourself by thinking, *They wouldn't have loaned me this money if they didn't think I could pay it back.* It's not the financial aid office's job to make that call. It's your responsibility. The lender knows you'll have no choice but to pay back what you owe, even if it means you won't be able to accept a low-paying dream job, buy a house, stay home with your kids, or enjoy a more peaceful adult life.

In Trap 4, we'll talk about choosing a major and a career path. I'm not saying everyone should just go for the big money. For one, not everyone is cut out to succeed in engineering, medicine, law, or corporate finance. But more importantly, living for money is a good way to wind up miserable, as money never satisfies those who love it (see Ecclesiastes 5:10). You need to pursue something you enjoy enough to put in the time and effort it takes to succeed. Something that's consistent with your talents, with how God has wired you, and something for which you can make enough money to have food to eat and to have a roof over your head. If that's French literature, so be it. But whatever major you choose, go into college with a realistic perspective of how much money you'll need to borrow — not just for one year, but all the way to graduation — and what kind of salary you're likely to earn after you graduate. Make sure it's a debt you'll be able to repay. I'm told that living like a pauper but doing what you love can be its own reward. But being chased by debt collectors? Not so much.

Why Can't We Just Forgive Student Loans?

That would be the equivalent of a trillion dollar bailout for the current generation of debtors. The money would have to come from the U.S. Treasury, which means it would be tacked on to the national debt (over eighteen trillion dollars and rising). In other words, the student debt of some U.S. residents would be passed on to all U.S. taxpayers and their children. How is that fair? Moreover, this would not address the underlying issues that led to the problem in the first place. Which means another generation of students would soon rise up who required the same assistance.

Instead, we need to help today's students and graduates pay off their loans as promptly as possible while helping tomorrow's students minimize or avoid student debt, or at least take on a debt load that's proportional to the salaries associated with their field of study.

The Bottom Line

It's up to you to exercise discernment when it comes to student loans. The nice folks at the financial aid office aren't your personal consultants; they work for the school. They aren't responsible for the loan offers you sign; you are. They won't live with the consequences of the choices you make; you will. So don't expect them to exercise the care and consideration that you must apply. "If you become wise, you will be the one to benefit. If you scorn wisdom, you will be the one to suffer" (Proverbs 9:12 NLT). Assuming "it's all just going to work out" — no matter how much debt you've racked up, no matter what your job prospects are — is naive and foolish.

But I've got good news: Getting a bachelor's degree doesn't need to cost you a fortune. That's what Trap 3 is about.

PART 2

MAKING SMART DECISIONS
KNOWING YOUR OPTIONS

SPEND A FORTUNE ON PRESTIGE (AND OTHER BAD IDEAS)

Let your head lead your heart

At this point you may be thinking, *Forget it. College isn't worth it. I can't afford it, and now that I see how student loans work, I want nothing to do with them.* That's what my friend Kyle's blue-collar parents told him. "College?" Kyle's dad scoffed. "You can't afford to go to college! Just work hard, and you'll be fine. Like your mom and me."

But that's wishful thinking. As I mentioned in Trap 1, in 1970 — when Kyle's dad was in his prime earning years — the vast majority of the middle-class workforce lacked any formal education beyond high school.[1] But today? If nothing else, Kyle needed a post–high school degree to signal to employers that he was worth hiring. If you're entrepreneurial or can get noticed through sheer brilliance, self-education, or a lucky break, more power to you. But people like Bill Gates, Steve Jobs, and Mark Zuckerberg are the exceptions that prove the rule.

Kyle had a knack for computer programming and, I'm happy to report, went to a good four-year college. Seven years out, he now makes $100,000 per year, owns a bigger home than his parents, and is two years away from paying off all his student debt. I'm not a big fan of student loans, but it'd be misleading to suggest that every borrower teeters on the verge of bankruptcy. If you racked up $15,000 in subsidized federal student loans, you'd be able to pay them all off in ten years with $160 per month.[2] That's not bad, if it buys you access to a rewarding career through which you can put your God-given abilities to work for the good of others.

The question is, How do you get a marketable degree without paying a fortune, especially if, like Kyle's, your parents can't afford to pick up the tab?

Entire books are written on how to choose a college.[3] My goal in this chapter is more specific: to help you get the best value for your dollar. I'll unpack three pitfalls to avoid in the college selection process and then offer some ideas on how to minimize the price tag without sacrificing quality.

The first pitfall is the idea that you should go to the "college of your dreams."

Beware of the "College of Your Dreams"

Disney and others have sold us on the idea that we should follow our dreams, whatever the cost. I'm all for pursuing dreams, but I've learned that success depends less on how strongly you believe and more on how smartly you proceed. Beware of making a college decision on the basis of an emotional impulse or a subjective impression. Some of the sales pitches colleges use aim at the heart, but they bypass the mind, discouraging prospective students from fully considering the price tag or the likelihood of success.

For example, one website I found boasts, "We believe college can be a reality for everyone, no matter your income or background." That sounds great ("If you can believe, you can achieve!"), but it *may* be a recipe for disaster. Remember that almost half of the people who start college never graduate, and two of the main reasons they don't are ... income and background. Similarly, a friend of mine once heard a vice president at a Christian college tell a group of prospective students' parents, "Some of you are wondering if you can afford to send your child here. What you need to ask yourself is whether you can afford *not* to." Is that an appeal based on logic and reason, or is it a manipulative scare tactic? I wish Christian colleges were immune to difficulties with student debt repayment, but they're not.[4]

Kelsey Griffith is an interesting case study. Her father, a paramedic, and her mother, a preschool teacher, earn modest incomes and have seven mouths to feed (Kelsey has four sisters). But that didn't stop Kelsey from choosing to attend Ohio Northern University, an expensive private college. Apparently, "she was won over by faculty and admissions staff members who urge students to pursue their dreams rather than obsess on the sticker price."[5] She graduated in 2012 with a marketing degree and $120,000 in debt.

Days before her commencement ceremony, she said, "I knew a private school would cost a lot of money. But when I graduate, I'm going to owe, like, $900 a month. No one told me that." Kelsey probably believed that borrowing lots of money was common. The truth is that only 10 percent of the class of 2012 completed their bachelor's degree with more than $49,000 in loans and only 0.3 percent managed to pile on a six-figure debt load.[6] Remember, it's *your* job to make sure you don't overborrow. Never expect a college to make that calculation for you. They have far less at stake than you do.

Kelsey is one of many who have been sucked into choosing a college for emotional, subjective reasons rather than clear-headed, objective criteria. Look, I've spent most of my life on college campuses, either as a student or professor. I know what it's like to walk across a beautiful campus and think, *This place is amazing.* But it's crucial that you let your head lead your heart in the choice of a college. It's too expensive a purchase to make any other way. Find a college that makes sense for you *and* that you love, but don't wait for a voice from heaven or a mystical feeling to seal the deal. And don't let yourself be overly distracted by amenities, sentimentality, local attractions, or where a good friend went. Look for an affordable school that offers a good education for whatever you plan to study.

Beware of Undermatching

Many students from lower-income backgrounds undermatch in their choice of college.[7] They choose a school that's below their academic abilities and accomplishments, one with less-prepared students and a lower graduation rate. At such a college they're not as likely to make the kinds of professional connections with professors and potential employers that can help them be successful. They're more likely to get dragged down by an underachieving crowd and fail to graduate. Outside of class, they don't experience the networking advantages that students from wealthier families typically enjoy. The clincher is that some of them end up spending too much for college and going into deep debt because the schools they choose don't have the money to provide them with the tuition assistance they need and would be given at more well-endowed universities.

Why does this happen? Because many of these students lack the support structure to knowledgeably guide them in their exploration of college choices. Let's face it, the world of college admissions can be complicated and intimating. Even more so when it comes to the selective, prestigious universities.

I'm hoping that many of you reading this book come from lower-income households. Or maybe you grew up in one, and now you're out on your own, trying to make a go at it, but knowing you need a degree. I want to help you get an education and the appropriate credentials to access the kinds of jobs that will give you social mobility. For the sake of our society, we need you to reach your potential. If you qualify for a Federal Pell Grant or a subsidized Federal Stafford loan, you're probably in this category. If neither of your parents went to college, you're probably in this category. Through no fault of your own, you're at a disadvantage in the insider's game of college admissions.

Collegedata.com: A Great Online Tool for Comparing Colleges

The website collegedata.com has a College Match tool that allows you to examine financial aid data at just about any college. You can see the number of financial aid applicants, the percentage of these who were found to have financial need, the percentage of students whose need was "fully met," and the "average percent of need met." You'll see the average awards broken down into need-based gift (grants), need-based self-help (loans and work-study), and merit-based gift (scholarships). You want the average need-based gift figure to be high.

These figures are available for all undergraduates and also for freshmen only. Look for differences — colleges sometimes dole out more grants and scholarships to freshmen than to other undergraduate students.[8] You don't want to be asked to shoulder a $12,000 bill the first year and an $18,000 bill each year thereafter. You want to be able to forecast your expenses for all four years.

The College Match tool lets you see the percentage of students who took out loans and the average indebtedness of a recent graduating class. (If you want to know the college's student loan default rate, you can find that on the NCES College Navigator site [nces. ed.gov/collegenavigator] mentioned in this chapter.) The College Match tool also allows you to search for colleges based on specific financial aid criteria. You can limit your search to colleges in up to sixteen states that have, for example, 10,000 students or less, meet at least 75 percent of applicants' financial need, and whose students graduate with an average debt load of $20,000 or less.

If that's you, here's my recommendation: Don't just apply to the community college down the street that you know you can get into. Apply to colleges that have strong programs in what you want to study *and* that have generous financial aid policies — even if they're selective and, on paper, expensive. At the National Center for Education Statistics College Navigator (nces.ed.gov/collegenavigator), you can find information about admissions at any college or university. If your SAT/ACT scores are above a college's twenty-fifth percentile, you've got a decent shot at getting in, though I wouldn't say you're a shoo-in. You should apply to several colleges, including a safety school, one where your SAT/ACT scores are above a college's seventy-fifth percentile.

The College Navigator also gives a window into a college's generosity in a way that complements what you can find at collegedata.com. When looking at a particular college, the College Navigator breaks down the "average net price by income" into five different groups, from the lowest income households to the highest, for each of the last three years. This lets you see what students from your family's income level were asked to pay, earn, or borrow (after scholarships and grants knocked down the total price tag). Apply to colleges where those with low incomes are paying much less than those with higher incomes. The more selective universities are often the wealthiest, and therefore the most generous in this respect. You can also ask your high school's guidance counselor or favorite teachers for college suggestions based on your SAT/ACT scores and grades. And take those tests twice to make sure you've done as well as you can.

If you have a decent chance of being accepted, don't reject a university because their website says tuition is crazy-high. The "average net price by income" for your income level is a better indicator. For example, for the 2012–2013 academic year, if your family's annual income ranged from $48,001 to $75,000, Duke University would have asked you to pay, earn, or borrow a little over $14,000. That's for everything—tuition, fees, room, board, books, and supplies. Yes, that's less than some public universities. Duke can afford to be this generous. Of course, it's tough to get into Duke. But the research demonstrates that when a student from a low-income background does well in high school, goes to a selective university, and receives a generous financial aid package, that student often does better in the long run than if he or she had gone to a less selective school.[9]

However, if your family is too wealthy to qualify for need-based financial aid, but your grades and test scores, like most of ours, aren't off the charts, you face another danger. The third pitfall is the opposite of the second: paying a fortune to attend a selective university in the hopes that the prestige will be worth the extra money.

Beware of Going into Debt for Prestige

There's a working assumption among many middle- and upper-class families that it's worth spending an arm and a leg to say you went to a prestigious university. We overestimate how important where we go to college is to employers. I'm all for students getting good grades and the best SAT/ACT test scores they can and then applying to colleges that have strong academic programs, but I don't see the need to take on massive debt to earn a college degree. At some point, the extra debt undermines whatever advantages you may have gained by attending a more elite university.

Before you tell me I'm contradicting what I said in the previous section, let me explain. Going to a college is like flying on an air plane: You aren't paying the same amount as the person sitting next to you, although you're getting basically the same service (much as I hate the dreaded middle seat). Colleges discount tuition for different students in different ways, but it boils down to a combination of *need* and *merit*. I discussed need in the previous section. Colleges try to help students from low-income families to the extent they can. Some colleges have more ability to do so than others because they have more money coming in from other sources, such as their endowment or their donors. With merit aid, they're comparing applicants to each other. At many private colleges, a large percentage of students get a few thousand dollars per year of merit aid, but only the very top students receive the big awards (anywhere from $10,000 per year to a full-ride).

FACTOID

A fall 2013 survey of eighteen- to twenty-four-year-old college students and hiring managers found that 45 percent of students believe a degree from a prestigious school is very or extremely important to make them more attractive to employers. By contrast, only 28 percent of hiring managers found this important.[10]

Let's go back to the example of Duke University. In 2012–2013 students whose family's annual income was in the $75,001–$110,000 range were asked to pay more than $25,000—quite a bit more than the $14,000 or so required of those students whose families earned

$48,001 – $75,000. Attending Duke for $14,000 a year is a great deal. But paying $25,000 per year or more? That's a different question. If your family's annual income is more than $110K, the cost is greater than $25K — up to an average of $45,034 for students from the wealthiest families. At some point, I don't care how great Duke is; it can't be worth it, especially if it means borrowing more than $10K extra each year.

Do you see what's happening? Low-income students who do well in high school can get great deals from schools wealthy enough to be generous to them — schools these students couldn't otherwise afford to attend. But middle-class students often get squeezed at these *same* universities because they don't qualify for need-based grants and they're not brilliant enough, athletic enough, or musically inclined enough to land much in the way of merit-based scholarships.

So if you can't qualify for generous need-based aid, don't assume you should attend the most selective university possible just so you can say you went there. Congrats on getting accepted by some big-name school, but go to your second choice if it means saving fifteen grand each year. Finances aside, attending the best college you can get into can backfire if you end up being among the weaker students. For example, if you plan to pursue something that's science, technology, engineering, or math related (known as the STEM fields) there's evidence that you'll do better as a great student at a good school than as a good student at a great school. Being a big fish in a small pond is the first of six ways we'll explore to get the most bang for your buck.

Getting the Most Bang for Your Buck

1. Consider the advantages of being a "big fish in a small pond." In his book *David and Goliath*, iconoclastic bestselling author Malcolm Gladwell compares STEM majors at both Hartwick College, a small private college in New York, and at über-prestigious Harvard University.[11] It's widely believed that plenty of high-paying jobs await STEM graduates after graduation. But the attrition rate of STEM students is higher than for other majors, meaning lots of students switch out of STEM fields into non-STEM disciplines.

STEM fields are challenging. There are clear, objective parameters for academic success. Your answers are either right or wrong. Math and science are like that.

Getting back to Hartwick and Harvard, I don't think I have to tell you which is the more selective school (no offense to Hartwick fans). The table below puts the students at each school into three buckets based on their math SAT scores. Just going off that one metric, notice that the weakest students at Harvard (581) are slightly stronger than the strongest students at Hartwick (569):

School	Top Third	Middle Third	Bottom Third
Harvard	753	674	581
Hartwick	569	472	407

But a curious thing happens when we look at the portion of STEM degrees earned by each group of students:

School	Top Third	Middle Third	Bottom Third
Harvard	53.4	31.2	15.4
Hartwick	55.0	27.1	17.8

At both colleges, more than half of the degrees are earned by the students whose math SAT scores were in the top third for that college. For Hartwick, that's not a huge surprise. If your math SAT score is 407, you might prefer a non-STEM major once you've experienced the rigors of calculus, physics, or engineering courses. But Harvard? Shouldn't *all* Harvard students be able to succeed in a STEM field if they just stick to it? Yet we see that at *both* colleges only about one in six (15 to 18 percent) of the STEM degrees granted went to those in the bottom third. It's not that Harvard's bottom third is dropping out. Harvard's graduation rate is above 95 percent. They're simply opting out of STEM fields.

Why? Being at the bottom of the pack is discouraging, especially for those accustomed to shining as the best and brightest. The moral of the story, says Gladwell, is that there are benefits to choosing a college where you will shine, even if it's (gasp) less reputable.

The Hartwick-Harvard comparison also resonates with my personal story. I was lazy for most of high school but enjoyed math and science. I got my act together during my senior year, but by then it was too late to impress colleges. I was planning to major in engineering. Selective Duke University rejected me and nonselective Alfred University accepted me. That "mishap" led to my graduating second in my class, landing immediate employment with IBM, and, three years later, securing acceptance into a top-five graduate school, the University of California at Berkeley. I discovered that a remarkable number of my peers at UC Berkeley also graduated from much lesser-known undergraduate programs, where they too had excelled.

2. You're more likely to pick up merit-based aid at a less selective college, since it's awarded based on how well you stack up against other applicants. My wife discovered this when she was accepted to both Whitman College in Walla Walla, Washington, and prestigious Stanford University in the heart of California's Silicon Valley. At Whitman she would have been one of their top incoming students, so they offered to pay almost all of her expenses. Stanford offered her the honor of attending, and little else. In the end, she chose Stanford, but only because her relatives were willing to foot most of the hefty bill. She had a great time and graduated with less than $10,000 in federal loans, which she quickly paid off after graduation. But had Grandpa and the gang not come through, her debt level would have easily been in the six-figure range. Not. Worth. It.

It's the person, not the pedigree, that makes the difference. Perhaps you're thinking, *You get what you pay for. Don't graduates of higher-ranked colleges do better in their careers than graduates of lower-ranked schools — even if they graduate with lower GPAs? And if so, aren't the selective colleges worth it, even if you can't qualify for need-based aid and they stick you with a huge bill?*

PayScale.com, a Seattle-based Internet company founded in 2002, has set out to answer this question, and they've received considerable publicity for their efforts. Using a mountain of self-reported earnings data from the alumni of some fifteen hundred four-year colleges, PayScale has been calculating the return on investment (ROI) for these colleges.[12] Here's how it works: If it costs $100,000 to get a degree from Elite U, and you end up earning $1,100,000 more over your career than if you hadn't attended college, then your ROI for attending Elite U is $1,000,000. (It's actually more complicated because PayScale also accounts for the opportunity cost—the amount of money you *could have earned* in the four to six years you spent going to Elite U.)

I understand the impulse to think of college as an investment, and I appreciate what PayScale is trying to do, but there are a few issues worth observing. First, since PayScale's salary figures are self-reported, they can't be verified. It's a bit like Wikipedia; accuracy is only as good as the crowd reporting the information. I would put greater confidence in the data from CollegeMeasures.org, though at the time of this writing such data is only available for a handful of states.[13] Second, if a college graduates a higher percentage of students who go into high-paying fields like engineering, computer programming, health care, and financial services, that college will rise to the top.[14] But that doesn't make the *college* better; it just means certain fields are more lucrative than others. We already knew that. And third—and here's the primary drawback—PayScale has no way to assess whether a student who *could have* gone to a more selective college *but didn't* actually comes out the worse for it.

However, that comparison has been done between the private, Ivy League University of Pennsylvania and middle-of-the-pack Penn State University.[15] At U Penn, 75 percent of students have a combined SAT score of more than 2030—something that's true of fewer than 25 percent of Penn State students.[16] You might think that students who picked Penn State over U Penn did so out of laziness or lack of ambition. But their future earnings ended up being about the same as their U Penn counterparts.[17]

The quality of your education, and how well you do after graduation, financially and otherwise, is primarily a function of *you*, not your alma mater.

Why? Because the quality of your education, and how well you do after graduation, financially and otherwise, is primarily a function of *you*, not your alma mater. It's the *person*, not the *pedigree*, that makes the biggest difference.[18] Notice that the students who could have gone to U Penn probably ended up being among the top students at Penn State, giving them the "big fish in the small pond" advantage we discussed earlier (not to mention the financial savings of being at a state university).

I'm not saying go to college anywhere. There are some real losers out there. If a college hands out degrees without making students earn them, run away. If it has been around for a while but can't point to successful graduates who are working and leading productive lives, move along. Some places are more interested in taking your money than in giving you a transformative educational experience that will prepare you for a career and a life. But you don't have to bankrupt yourself to get a great education. As long as you avoid the duds, *that* you go to college is more important than *where* you go (assuming you graduate). Which means you have every right—and responsibility—to stick to a budget and shop for value.

Is It Worth Going into Debt to Be at a Christian College?

I completed my undergraduate at a secular private college, did my graduate work at a large public university, and am going into my tenth year as a professor at a Christian institution. So I've seen it all, and I'm happy to report that Christians can thrive in either environment. That said, I appreciate the value of a distinctively Christian higher education, especially as I consider the future of my own children. I think it *is* worth paying more to get faculty who teach their subjects from a Christian worldview and care deeply about their students and to have a campus environment that's supportive of your values. Before you dismiss Christian colleges on the basis of list price, you should understand that significant discounts are not uncommon. Consult the websites I mentioned earlier.

But is it worth going into debt to attend a Christian college? It depends on your future earnings prospects and how much debt we're talking about. It also depends on how you're wired and where you'd be most likely to succeed. I can't imagine a scenario in which private loans are ever worth it (see Trap 5). But what about $10,000 to $20,000 in subsidized federal loans (over four years) if you're a hardworking, academically motivated, responsible student who would get lost at a huge university but who would thrive in a nurturing environment with smaller classes? An alternative would be to spend two years at a community college followed by two years at a Christian college.

3. Set a budget. Together with your family, determine the amount of money you can afford to pay per year for college. And have a plan to graduate as quickly as possible. I recommend that students not borrow much, if any, money as freshmen for three reasons: (1) The interest accrues for a longer period of time (unless the loan is subsidized—see Trap 5); (2) many students change their major that first year (pushing back the finish line); and (3) starting with debt usually means ending with *big* debt. Can't afford that first year? Why not head to a community college, pay for it with cash, and transfer your credits elsewhere?

If you don't decide what you can afford, the colleges to which you apply will be happy to do that for you—though you might not like their answers. You'll complete the FAFSA, which will compute your Expected Family Contribution (EFC). Unless a college's total price is below your EFC, you'll be required to pay at least as much as your EFC and probably more. The most prestigious colleges will require financial aid applicants to complete the CSS/Financial Aid PROFILE.[19] The PROFILE takes a deeper look at your family's assets. For example, my wife qualified for a Federal Pell Grant and subsidized federal loans, but Stanford still required her to pay an arm and a leg. Why? Because the federal formula only looks at annual income, but Stanford (using the PROFILE) was also looking at her family's substantial home equity.

Whether your college uses the FAFSA or the PROFILE, don't expect your EFC to necessarily be within your budget. It might not be. That's why it's good to have both a budget and knowledge of your EFC in advance.[20]

Okay, so setting an upper limit on price is important, but what about quality? After all, two colleges may both charge you $20,000 per year, but at one school you're paying for great professors, classrooms, libraries, and labs, and at the other school you're paying for a football stadium, a deluxe cafeteria, high-rise apartment housing, and an upscale student center.

4. Assess instructional quality. Colleges collect money in many ways—tuition and fees, room and board, government funds (even at private schools), rental income, donations, and earnings on their endowments. And they spend money in many ways—instruction, administration/overhead, and student services are the three biggies. How can you know if a college is prioritizing education and training rather than amenities or a bloated bureaucracy? One way is to look at the quality of the academic and professional resources (the buildings where classes are held, the classrooms themselves, the library, the laboratories, the career center, and so on) in comparison to the social and recreational amenities (the cafeteria, student union, football stadium, fitness center, and so forth). Go on a campus tour and see how the tour guide "sells" the college. You can get a rough idea of what a school values by how it presents itself, by how it seeks to attract prospective students. A final way is to query the students themselves to see what they value. You're only getting a snapshot, so take it with a grain of salt, but ask them about their study habits, what their professors are like, and what support systems are in place to help students succeed academically and professionally. Observe students in a class during a campus visit and try to get a sense of the overall culture. Is academics important, or is the social scene front and center?

You probably want to be at a college that looks nice, has well-maintained buildings and grounds, and offers students at least some recreational programming and common amenities (like a fitness center). I don't blame you. I would too. It's a matter of degree. Remember what I said earlier: Focus on what's essential, not peripheral. If you borrow to live like a professional when you're a student, you might end up living like a student when you're a professional.

The Delta Cost Project website (www.tcs-online.org/Home.aspx) lets you see how colleges receive their money and where they spend it on a per-student basis. So does the CollegeMeasures.org site I mentioned earlier. The Chronicle of Higher Education has a website called College Completion (collegecompletion.chronicle.com), which, in addition to posting graduation rates, reports how much money a college spends educating a student from his or her first day through graduation. It also shows how much financial aid the average student receives and how much endowment money is available per student.

> **If you borrow to live like a professional when you're a student, you might end up living like a student when you're a professional.**

Assuming a college has the right priorities, a higher "total cost of instruction" (the figure listed on a college's website) shouldn't scare you away if the "net price" (what you're ultimately asked to pay, earn, or borrow) is within your budget. In fact, a high cost of instruction can be a good thing if the college is investing in giving its students a high-quality education (functional classrooms; smaller class sizes; state-of-the-art laboratories; useful online instructional resources; a variety of educational programs; qualified, accessible faculty; and so on).

To put it bluntly, you want as much instructional spending for as little of your money as possible. Generous private schools can be great. But so are many community colleges and public universities.

5. *Consider starting at a community college and finishing at a public university.* This is a well-worn and less expensive path toward a bachelor's degree. It's less expensive because a large portion of your instructional costs are carried by the taxpayers. One of the biggest weaknesses with large public universities is that the class sizes are often enormous the first two years. You can beat the system by taking as many lower-level classes as possible at a community college,

where you'll often find reasonable class sizes and dedicated, egoless faculty who are passionate about teaching. The flip side is that it's sometimes difficult to get into all the classes you want. If your path to a bachelor's degree is delayed, it can end up costing you more in terms of the time you lose getting your bachelor's degree instead of earning money.

Another concern is that the process of transferring credits from a community college to a four-year university can be complicated. The personnel at the registrar's offices (I'm told) are sometimes less than knowledgeable. So do your research carefully to make sure you don't take classes you'll need to *retake* at a four-year university. Some states are now offering guaranteed transfer programs, where anyone who earns an Associate in Arts from a community college is automatically accepted into a program in the state university system.

By the way, a great way to get more instructional excellence for your dollar at a four-year state university is to get into their honors program, assuming they have one. Honors programs allow qualified, motivated students to interact with professors in smaller, specialized classes that enhance learning and develop creativity, critical thinking, and communication skills. They also connect you to a peer group of achievers who, together with the faculty with whom you develop relationships and the thousands of alumni from that school who've gone before you, form the seedbed for a professional network (people who can assist you in landing career opportunities throughout your life).

6. Consider "$10K-BA"-type options. Texas and Wisconsin, in response to a challenge issued by entrepreneur-turned-philanthropist Bill Gates, are among a growing number of states trying to roll out bachelor's degree programs whose total cost through graduation is about $10,000. These programs leverage online instruction and efficiency measures such as dual enrollment in the latter part of high school. Most of the programs so far are in applied fields like science, technology, engineering, math, business, management, and health care. But online liberal arts programs are also emerging.[21]

Some claim that a stripped-down, bare-bones degree is of lesser value. As a professor, I agree that face-to-face instruction has distinct advantages. But I think the critics miss a larger point. While higher instructional costs generally lead to a higher-quality education, the money must come from somewhere. Well-endowed private universities are few and far between. The federal government is neck-deep in debt, state governments are spending elsewhere, and family incomes have been flat or declining for at least a decade. Meanwhile the cost of higher education is rising faster than the rate of inflation, and the student debt burden at graduation is rising faster than starting salaries.

With the majority of the public believing that higher education is both essential *and* overpriced, the environment is ripe for alternative models to arise.[22] In 2011, it was reported that online enrollment was growing at a rate ten times faster than that of all higher education.[23] The "$10K-BA" models, with their low price and focus on career preparation, offer the promise of social mobility to those who might have a job and kids or to those who, for whatever reason, can't afford to drop everything to become a traditional college student.

The flip side is that to do well as an online student you need to be motivated, disciplined, and willing to seek assistance from assigned mentors and classmates available via Internet chat sessions and the like. In some of these programs, competencies are assessed whenever you are ready, allowing you to progress toward graduation at your own pace. You pay in three- or six-month intervals. This approach, known as competency-based education, was pioneered by Western Governors University (WGU), an online, accredited, private, nonprofit university founded in 1997 by nineteen state governors. You graduate when you've completed all of the necessary assessments in your field. At WGU, you pay a flat fee of $3,000 to $4,000 every six months. The average student graduates in two and a half to three years, paying $15,000 to $25,000, total.

I recommend staying away from the for-profit online schools because they're usually more expensive and have abysmal graduation and student loan default rates. But I anticipate that nonprofit online programs, which lower costs by requiring less contact with professors, less need for physical buildings, and little to no auxiliary student services while letting students move through coursework at their own pace, will grow in popularity. The stigma associated with going to college this way will decrease as employers increasingly consider prospective employees on the basis of what they know and can do and not on where or how they got their training.

The Bottom Line

If a four-year college is right for you, you *can* get your bachelor's degree without breaking the bank. But to do so, you'll need to avoid the three pitfalls we discussed: paying through the roof for the "college of your dreams," undermatching, and going into deep debt for prestige. Instead, look for schools that invest in education but that won't charge you a fortune. While Christian schools offer distinct advantages and aren't necessarily unaffordable, community colleges, public universities, and online programs can provide cost-effective avenues for earning your degree.

Money shouldn't be the only factor in your decision. If a college would cost a little more but give you a better all-around experience — academically, socially, spiritually, professionally — go for it. Just remember that money is *a* factor. Blissful ignorance can lead to long-term regret.

CHOOSE YOUR MAJOR ON A WHIM

Know what you're getting into

Selecting a college strategically is huge; it can save you a small fortune. But how much is riding on the choice of your major? Do some majors increase your chances of finding a job and commanding a high salary? Do other majors condemn you to a job at Starbucks and living in your parents' basement?

Let's get one thing clear: Salary prospects—though worth knowing about—should not drive your choice of a college major, especially if you're fresh out of high school; unattached to a job, spouse, or children; and have your whole life in front of you. If you're older, already working, married, or have children, it's understandable that you'd view college more as a chance to raise your earning prospects than anything else. But even then, if all you do is "go for the money," you're not likely to find satisfaction (see Ecclesiastes 5:10).

What factors should you consider when choosing a major? With any field you go into, the only way to achieve excellence is to spend a lot of time doing it. So choose something you like, because you're more likely to put in the time. But to be really good in your field, you also need a measure of natural inclination. So pick a major that leverages your talents. The more easily something comes to you, the more quickly you'll see improvement.

I like playing sports. The more I do it, the better I get. To a point. Sadly for me, the improvement has never been huge. My athletic prowess is never going to put food on my table. But writing? It took me a long time to get a book published. But I received strong encouragement from several of my professors in college and even placed first in a national writing contest during my junior year. When I put in the time to become a better writer, I made more improvement than I ever did in sports (or music or art or working with my hands). I found the same thing to be true in math, science, and teaching. Throughout high school and college, I was always tutoring other students. People told me they understood the material after I had explained it. And I loved contributing to their learning.

So what do I do today? I'm a professor, a writer, and a public speaker. People actually pay me to do these things. What a deal! I've sought to build my life around the way God wired me. I encourage you to do the same. Trying to chase big money in the choice of your college major is a mistake many students today are making, leaving them frustrated, if not failing, in majors that aren't right for them. But other students are making the opposite mistake: ignoring the job prospects of their major and failing to consider their likely future salary in how they fund their college education.

Let's begin by discussing the importance of understanding your field of interest when you declare a major. Then we'll explore how much your choice of major impacts what you end up doing after college, how much you get paid for it, and how likely you are to wind up flipping burgers.

Understanding Your Field of Interest

Maybe you aren't sure what you want to be when you grow up. That's common for eighteen-year-olds coming out of high school. I'm all for personal discovery at college, but the flip side is that if finances dictate that you must graduate in four years, it helps to go in with a plan. That's especially true if you select a major that has a lot of course requirements. Perhaps you're bright and can handle higher than average course loads. Maybe you're bringing in advanced placement or International Baccalaureate credit, or you've already taken some classes at a community college. If so, you may have more latitude to explore a few options before declaring a major (while still graduating in four years).

But for most of you, it's risky to wait until you're paying tuition before giving serious thought to your major. It's true that most students switch majors, but it's also true that most take five or more years to complete a four-year degree, and at significant additional expense. It's best to use your high school years to learn as much as possible about your long-term interests and talents. Consider your accomplishments, because they provide an objective measure of your skill in certain areas: writing, math, science, or whatever. Take the time to understand what different jobs and careers entail. If you want to be a physical therapist, find out what it involves on a day-to-day basis. Don't just think, *That sounds cool!* Spend a day shadowing someone, research the field, and really look into it. What skills, background, and experience are needed to succeed in school and in the workforce? The more overlap between who you are and what it takes to be effective in the line of work you're pursuing, the greater your chances for long-term success.

> **Don't just think, *That sounds cool!* Spend a day shadowing someone, research the field, and really look into it.**

Too late for you to go back to high school? It's still in your interest to become more confident about what you want to study and your likelihood of success before enrolling in a four-year college. If you're told you need to take math or English classes before you enroll in courses that count toward graduation, know that your chances of earning a bachelor's degree in six years or fewer are about one in three.[1] Be realistic. Count the cost. Test the waters before jumping in (for example, by fulfilling any precollege-level courses online or at a community college as a part-time student while keeping your full-time job). Consider alternatives, like getting an associate's degree first or pursuing a skilled trade (see Trap 1).

Last, find out the significance of a bachelor's degree and what starting salary you can expect to earn with a degree in a particular field. The Bureau of Labor Statistics is a great resource. Just go to the website (www.bls.gov) and type in the name of a job. You'll find the median salary, the entry-level education, the number of current jobs, and the outlook for job growth in that field. The Bureau also has a Fastest Growing Occupations chart (www.bls.gov/ooh/fastest-growing.htm), which lists the current number of jobs, the anticipated number of openings in ten years, and the current median annual salary for each of the designated occupations.

While making money shouldn't be a consuming passion, you have to live in the real world. "Likely future salary" is a piece of information that thousands of former students with high amounts of student debt wish they had known when they started college. For example, I've met biology graduates who were surprised both by how hard it was to find work and by the less than stellar annual salaries they were offered ($30,000–$35,000 in 2013). What they should have known going in is that a bachelor's degree in biology is often a stepping-stone to an advanced degree, such as one earned in medical school or in a research-based graduate program. That's where you get the larger return on investment.

But maybe you're wondering, *How much does my major really matter? Can't I study history and wind up in management, or study Spanish and land a job in marketing?*

Does It Matter What You Study?

Yes, it's possible to study one subject and end up working in an entirely different field, either right after college or five to ten years down the road. To keep your options open, differentiate yourself by picking up skills, professional work experiences, and extracurricular activities while going through college. Be creative, resourceful, and willing to step out of your comfort zone to discover ways you can add value to different kinds of organizations. Don't expect anything to be handed to you. Develop a track record that can interest a variety of prospective employers.

Some employers want to hire people with particular skills or specialized knowledge. This happens more often in the applied disciplines, such as engineering, computer science, architecture, nursing, or education. New hires are required to have specific abilities from the get-go; otherwise these organizations will have to train them, which is usually expensive and time-consuming (and, frankly, increasingly rare). So they narrow their search to those with a bachelor's degree in a discipline that imparts the technical abilities needed to be successful in their company or industry.

Other employers take a broader approach. They're looking to hire intelligent people with a bachelor's degree in just about anything—including those with a technical background, as these majors are known for cultivating analytical problem solvers. If such graduates have also developed good communication, leadership, and teamwork skills, they're great catches for virtually anyone.

One of the best ways to hedge your bets in an uncertain job market is to declare a major in two different areas. This is a great option if you have advanced placement or International Baccalaureate units. A double major immediately makes you a more interesting candidate. It demonstrates ambition, hard work, and perseverance to complete not just one but *two* majors. If your majors are related (e.g., electrical engineering and physics, philosophy and English), it might not require too many extra courses. That's also the case if the majors you're declaring have relatively few required courses.

If your interests are broad or eclectic, it's also fine to pursue a double major in two very different fields. For example, you could major in a humanities discipline as well as something practical like marketing, finance, or computer science. A good humanities degree trains you in critical thinking, problem solving, and communication—all of which are foundational competencies in all career paths. Your other degree could give you the skills that many employers would find immediately useful, for example, advertising, sales, or web design. Of course, the downside is that completing two very different majors can mean taking lots of courses, which for many students means five years or insanely busy summers. But the upside is that you'll have significant depth and breadth once you graduate. That should give you more options and greater versatility over the course of your career.

What about Financial Prospects?

Many students feel torn between what they love and perhaps do well and what they think can earn them a lot of money someday. It's no secret that financial prospects loom large for college students these days. In a 2012 survey conducted with thousands of incoming college freshmen, four out of five (81 percent) students identified "being very well-off financially" as a very important objective.[2] Engineering majors, for example, are exploding in popularity because of the perception that a pile of cash is waiting at the end of the college tunnel. Meanwhile, fewer students seem to be declaring majors in fields like English, philosophy, and foreign languages.

The recession and the high cost of college have forced your generation to view college primarily as a vocational training ground and less as a place to learn for the sake of learning. And there is some evidence that humanities majors have more difficulty landing that first job than those in applied majors. To make things worse, when they do find work, it's usually at a lower salary.

I mentioned a 2013 survey in Trap 1, which found that more than four in ten four-year college graduates described their employment as a job that doesn't require a four-year degree.[3] What I didn't mention is that this same survey found that while three out of four graduates in math, physics, engineering, and computer science were in jobs that require four-year degrees, only slightly more than half (54 percent) of language, literature, and social sciences majors and less than half (43 percent) of visual and performing arts majors could say the same. Similarly, a 2013 study from Georgetown University found that recent graduates whose degrees had high technical, business, or health care content were both less likely to be unemployed and more likely to be earning higher salaries than graduates in the arts, humanities, and architecture. Starting salaries for those with bachelor's degrees ranged from $28,000 (anthropology and archaeology) to $58,000 (mechanical engineering).[4]

Supply and demand play a role. For example, not to pick on anyone, but just shy of 109,000 degrees were awarded in 2012 for psychology—a 12 percent increase in just two years—although the

Bureau of Labor Statistics (BLS) reported that only 160,000 psychology jobs existed in 2012. By contrast, approximately 80,000 engineering degrees were awarded in 2012, although the BLS reported more than 270,000 jobs in civil engineering alone. Of course, psychology graduates can get into many other fields, such as forensics, law, and human resources, but the point remains: The number of new graduates in a discipline, relative to the number of job openings, is going to have an impact on the unemployment rate and starting salaries of those new graduates. Part of why visual and performing arts graduates have more trouble finding work than engineering graduates is that we've been graduating more of them *every year* since the year 2000.[5]

If engineering, math, and computer science majors earn good money, why aren't they more popular? They are, for freshmen, but they have a high attrition rate, as we discussed in the last chapter. They require some talent and *a lot* of hard work and discipline. Professors in these subjects are known to grade their students according to exacting, objective standards (and, yes, there's some evidence that on average they give lower grades).[6]

So here's the deal: If you're not strong in math and science, don't pursue a STEM field. No biggie. Choosing a major for the money, and then being unsuccessful, costs you more than choosing something you'd do well from the get-go. You have plenty of other options. For example, business, accounting, and education all impart marketable skills, and new graduates in these fields have relatively low unemployment. Don't worry—if your heart is in the liberal arts, there *are* ways to land employment. I'll come back to this a bit later.

If you *are* strong in math, physics, or computers, and you like these subjects, go for it. You'll probably have many open doors throughout your lifetime—and not just with technical employers. But there is a danger in overspecializing.

Andrew's Story

At the large state university I attended, we had more than a hundred majors to choose from, ranging from biology to middle and south Asian studies to philosophy and engineering. Switching majors midstream was not uncommon. I saw economics majors find history more interesting. Many of my friends started off in engineering, motivated by the lucrative market, only to discover it wasn't their passion.

I originally had doubts about wanting to double-major in international relations and economics since it didn't equate to a specific job. Then I realized that a major is about pursuing your interests and exploring the range of opportunities that exist after graduation. It's liberating to not be locked into one set thing.

Since entering the job market, I've found that many companies don't consider your major to be a make or break for the position you're pursuing. Instead, the experience you gained outside of the classroom can be the difference between an offer letter and a rejection email. My position as student body president was what landed me a job at an influential political organization in Washington, D.C., not the papers I wrote in my two majors.

A Warning to Techies: Don't Overspecialize

If you're a techie, you may be eating this up: *Yes! I don't want to waste my time with courses that aren't practical. I just want to learn things that I'll actually need to know when I get out.* The flip side is that the job you land after college may not be what you do for the rest of your life. Even if it is, career advancement usually has more to do with nontechnical skills than with any facts, figures, or computer programming languages you've mastered.

In his excellent book *College (Un)bound*, Jeff Selingo tells the story of David Muir, his college roommate and fellow journalism major. Mr. Muir is currently the anchor for *ABC World News*. When asked how his major prepared him for his career, Muir pointed out that the technology he learned in college (videotape and reel-to-reel audio) is now obsolete. But, Muir said, "the greater lessons I carry with me today are the other classes—the critical thinking, questioning public policy, forming arguments, and the discussions that put what we learned in the broader context of where the world is heading. We're in such an attention-deficit culture now that there is a premium on people who can take a step back, dissect an issue, spend some time on it, and write about it." At *ABC World News*, Muir works alongside plenty of non-journalism majors. He reflects, "We all majored in what we were interested in. The curiosity and the willingness to adapt are more important than what the degree is in."[7] I couldn't agree more. If what you gain from your major is a passion for learning, an inquisitiveness and ability to discover answers and put them into a broader context, you'll do well in many lines of work.

I've been teaching engineering students at the college level for ten years now. It's not uncommon for them to feel that their English, speech, and other general education classes are a waste of time, a distraction from the things they "need to know how to do." But that's a narrow, short-sighted, and ultimately foolish perspective. The reality is that you need both technical knowledge and soft skills to be successful in an engineering, a scientific, or a medical line of work. Being able to work with people, communicate well both verbally and in writing, deliver an engaging presentation, pick out the main points in a journal article or book, and differentiate between fact and opinion—these are skills that rigorous, well-structured general education classes impart. They come in handy no matter what you do. It's obvious to their employers when graduates lack these skills. It prevents them from advancing professionally. In worst-case scenarios, it can cost them their jobs.

Colleges sometimes add new specialized majors in fields that are supposed to be up-and-coming. For example, I recently read about programs in hospital financing, casino management, and pharmaceutical marketing.[8] The idea is to grab vocationally oriented students eager to get in on the ground floor of what could become a growing market. Health care is definitely a growing industry, and marketing is a perennial need, but *pharmaceutical marketing*?

Why not major in biology and minor in marketing (or vice versa), while taking some good general education courses too? That broadens your options after graduation. If the skills you develop for one career are applicable in another, you'll likely find yourself in a good place. If you don't develop a broad set of skills at college, you're selling yourself short. And you're missing out on an important aspect of what college is meant to be.

How can you tell if a major is too specialized? Do some Internet research on the major you're considering. There are some forty-five hundred degree-granting institutions. If only a handful offer the program you're considering, that's a warning sign. Next, identify whether the schools that have the major have a large or small program. Find out how long the major has been around. Has it been growing? What evidence exists that a degree in *that* major is necessary to get the job you want? Might a broader major work just as well, or better? Generally, graduate school is the time to specialize.

Caveat: Ignore everything I just said if you're already working full-time and your boss says, "I'll give you a $15,000 raise if you pass these five classes, which I'll pay you to take." That's old-fashioned professional development at its best!

If You Major in the Liberal Arts

If your heart is in the liberal arts, I've got good news. Though it helps to love the work for its own sake, it's not all doom and gloom when it comes to your salary prospects. Research shows that your salary — which might begin on the lower side — is likely to climb about as high as that of your peers in fields like nursing, education, and forensics over the course of your career.[9] Here are a few suggestions to give you a leg up in a tough environment:

1. Develop hard skills outside the classroom. Learn to edit and perhaps design websites, take good photographs, and use Microsoft Office products and Photoshop. Pick up summer work experiences, especially ones that let you take on responsibilities and demonstrate leadership. Take classes in practical fields like marketing, communication, and journalism, perhaps earning a minor in an outside field, or even a double major.

2. Show initiative. With the Internet, it's never been easier to start building a showcase of your work. If you're an English major, can you start a blog, review books (many publishers will send them to you for free), or write for your college's newspaper? Look for ways to get experience in areas such as public relations and communication, which are essential to every organization. Join your college's speech and debate team. Pursue an internship with a magazine, newspaper, or book publisher.

3. Talk to your professors about possible career tracks. Find out what you can do to differentiate yourself so your résumé stands out. Are there certain kinds of work or volunteer experience that would be particularly strategic to have? Is there a professional organization that has a student chapter you could join to learn more about career tracks, meet people, and hear about opportunities? The annual fee is usually low, and you can develop leadership experience by serving as an officeholder. Are there conferences you can attend? Admission is typically inexpensive (or free) for undergraduates. If there is a fee, they'll often waive it if you volunteer at the event.

4. Choose professors and classes that are rigorous. Don't just think about protecting your grade point average; that's less important to employers than most students think. It's about developing your skills for the long haul so you're the kind of person employers want, not just when you graduate, but ten and twenty years later. Avoid the trendy, fluffy courses that are becoming popular in some liberal arts programs.[10] Courses with terms like *race*, *gender*, and *sex* in the description are often more about political indoctrination than deep learning, which limits what majors like Women's Studies, Feminist Studies, Chicano Studies, and African-American Studies can do for your career (especially at the undergraduate level). You want courses that get you reading the authors who have shaped our civilization and require you to interact with important themes through writing substantive papers, participating in class discussions, and giving presentations. That's how you learn, grow, and get value from your education.

By the way, a liberal arts degree is a great foundation for entry into the business world. Skills like critical thinking and communication are particularly helpful in management contexts — and in getting promoted. You'd be surprised how many CEOs got their training in the liberal arts. Carly Fiorina, the former CEO of Hewlett-Packard, majored in medieval history and philosophy. American Express CEO Ken Chenault was a history major. JPMorgan Chase CEO James Dimon was a psychology and economics major. Successful businessman and former Massachusetts governor Mitt Romney was an English major. CNN and TBS founder Ted Turner was a classics major.[11] Other examples could be multiplied.

Keep two things in mind. First, future earnings tend to be a function of what industry you enter more than what your major was. If Sarah is a history major but ends up as a manager in a Fortune 500 company, she's going to make a lot more money than if she became a college professor (I'd know). Second, how far you go in your field is a function of your accomplishments and choices. The leaders I listed above are all intelligent and ambitious. There's a good chance they'd have been successful no matter what they studied. What matters is that they chose majors they liked and did them well. And I think it helped that their undergraduate degrees were broad, teaching them to think critically, solve problems, and communicate clearly. That learning became the catalyst for their future success, especially their ability to lead others.

As we wind down this chapter, let's shift gears and talk about how you can develop the skills that employers value, regardless of your major.

Developing the Skills That Employers Value

The bad news is that employers today are complaining about the quality of new college graduates. The good news is that by intentionally developing the skills and habits that many new graduates lack, you'll have a leg up in a competitive job market. So what are some common deficiencies cited by employers? Poor communication, interpersonal, and critical thinking skills and lack of creativity, motivation, and professionalism. For example, hiring managers say that half of new graduates entering the workforce aren't prepared to prioritize from among multiple job-related tasks.[12]

Can I be honest with you? Part of the problem is that many students aren't working hard in college. So they're not learning much, and they're not developing a work ethic that employers find essential for success. In 1961, full-time college students studied twenty-four hours per week. Fifty years later, in 2011, that figure was down to twelve hours per week. Both students who work side jobs and students who don't are studying less. A lot of the extra time goes into partying, video games, and Internet surfing.[13] We're paying a hefty price for it. A landmark research study found that almost half of college students (45 percent) are not making any statistically significant improvement in critical thinking, analytical reasoning, problem solving, and writing during their first two years of college. And 36 percent fail to do so over four years.[14]

How can you be sure to improve your intellectual abilities during your college years? Take classes with rigorous requirements, from faculty with high expectations, and spend lots of time studying (closer to twenty-four hours per week than twelve per week). Makes sense, right? You get out of your education what you put into it.

Interestingly, the researchers found that liberal arts students made "significantly higher gains in critical thinking, complex reasoning, and writing skills over time than students in other fields of study." That's probably because they read and write so much for their classes. But the researchers also found that "the field of study matters less than how much you work in the major ... Math and science majors don't write or read much for their classes, but they show gains in critical thinking because they spend the most hours studying ... It doesn't matter what these students focus on as long as they focus on it in a rigorous way."[15] In other words, if you want to grow in your critical thinking and reasoning skills, choose a major you like and can succeed in, work hard, be focused, and aim high.

A 2013 survey conducted by Chegg, Inc., asked hiring managers what they looked for in the résumés of new graduates.[16] Three items stood out:

- initiative/leadership (93 percent of hiring managers)
- participation in extracurricular activities related to one's field of study (91 percent of hiring managers)
- completion of a formal internship (82 percent of hiring managers)

There you have it. The second one is interesting, because the Chegg survey found that students were *twice* as likely to be involved in extracurricular activities *not* related to their field of study than ones that are.

On the flip side, it turns out that some of the things students *think* are important to employers really aren't:[17]

- 77 percent of students think professional or personal connections in their field of interest are important in getting a job; only 52 percent of hiring managers agreed. (That's still a majority—we'll discuss networking in Trap 8.)
- 68 percent of students think a high grade point average is very or extremely important for landing a job; only 48 percent of hiring managers agree. (A mixture of mostly B's and A's is fine. Beyond that, it doesn't really matter, unless you're going to graduate school.)

Here are three more things you can do to stand out to prospective employers:

1. Dive deep into a research project or a capstone course during your senior year. Group projects are great opportunities to develop research, communication, team-building, and leadership skills.

2. Develop an online portfolio of your work. Some colleges now require students do this using commercial software packages such as Livetext (www.livetext.com). An online portfolio is different from a transcript or résumé. It's a growing record of projects you've completed and key papers you've written, along with the courses you've taken and the grades you've earned (ideally, as compared to the average grade your professor gave in that class).[18] An online portfolio can later be shared with potential employers with hyperlinks, allowing them to check out your work.

3. Get on LinkedIn. It's like a Facebook for professional networking. As you complete specific courses in your major or develop particular skills like Microsoft Word, PowerPoint, Excel, Photoshop, editing, research, or whatever, you can add them to your profile. Professors and employers can write recommendations for you or endorse you as having the specific skills you list. And it's all preserved for the world to see. When you apply for full-time jobs, it's almost guaranteed that employers will check if you're on LinkedIn. By the way, they'll also look for you on Facebook, Twitter, and other social media sites to see how you're presenting yourself. So it's a good idea to keep your online image clean.

The Bottom Line

Choose a major you enjoy and in which you have the capacity to excel. Learn as much as you can about your field of interest—the job prospects, the starting salaries, the skills needed to succeed, how likely you are to need a graduate degree—before you start paying tuition. On the whole, job openings and salaries are currently most desirable in business, technical, and health care-related fields, but the truth is, you can succeed in the workforce with a degree in just about any major. What makes a difference?

- quality work
- passion and curiosity
- resilience, perseverance, flexibility, and a commitment to lifelong learning
- communication and critical thinking skills

- demonstrations of leadership, personal initiative, and professionalism
- relevant work experiences

We'll talk more in Trap 6 about the work experiences you can pursue *during* college that will help you launch a rewarding career *after* college. But first we need to make sense of the byzantine world of financial aid.

TRAP 5

STUDENT LOANS ARE ALWAYS WORTH IT

Develop awareness and exercise foresight

You've probably heard that student loans are "good debt" because you stand to earn more with a bachelor's degree than without one. That's true overall, but it's not true for every student. Even if loans help you get through college, it makes sense to keep your balance as low as you can. Why start your professional life deeper in the hole than necessary?

Financial aid is offered annually by the college or university you attend based on your Expected Family Contribution (EFC) as calculated by the Federal Application for Free Student Aid (FAFSA).[1] But you get to decide which parts of the financial aid package you accept or decline. You'll be a smarter customer if you know the differences between federal and private loans, what it means for a loan to be subsidized, and why fixed interest rates are preferable. By the time you get to the end of this chapter, you'll be able to estimate the future monthly payment associated with a particular loan. Don't worry. Even if you hate numbers, with the help of a calculator, spreadsheet, and the Internet, the math is totally doable! I'll explain what terms like *forbearance* and *deferment* mean. And we'll discuss the merits of loan products that colleges often pitch to parents.

Loans should be your last resort when it comes to paying for college.

But before we get to the particulars of student loans, let me walk you through how financial aid offices decide how much and what types of financial aid they're going to offer you. That way you'll see why loans should be your last resort when it comes to paying for college.

How Financial Aid Offices Determine Their Offers

The financial aid office at each college starts with your cost of attendance (COA)—an estimate of tuition and fees, plus room and board, plus the cost of books, supplies, and transportation.[2] Your COA will be lower, for example, if you're living at home with relatives than if you're planning to live on campus. The difference between your COA and EFC is defined as your *demonstrated financial need*. Note that your COA will vary from college to college, but your EFC is fixed for a given year.

For any college:
Demonstrated Financial Need =
Cost of Attendance (COA) –
Expected Family Contribution (EFC)

There is a rule here: *Under no circumstances can you receive more need-based aid than the amount of your demonstrated financial need.* For example, if your COA is $20,000, and your EFC is $8,000, you're eligible for up to $12,000 of *need-based* aid. Anything beyond $12,000 that the college may want to give you would have to be in the form of *merit-based* aid.

Need-based aid includes grants, work-study, and loans. Grants are known as "gift aid"; work-study and loans are collectively called "self-help aid." This distinction is helpful—grants represent money that doesn't have to be repaid; work-study represents the opportunity to earn money toward your COA; loans represent borrowed money that must be repaid with interest.

Merit-based aid, in contrast, refers to scholarships awarded by the college. Maybe you have a higher SAT or ACT score than most of the college's other applicants. Maybe you're a great singer, and you agree to sing in one or more of the university's choirs. Maybe the basketball coach has recruited you to play for the team. Unlike need-based aid, which has an upper limit defined by your demonstrated financial need (COA minus EFC), the only upper limit on merit-based aid is the college's COA. If you're accomplished or talented enough, a college can cover your entire COA, regardless of your EFC (e.g., a full-ride scholarship).[3]

More typically, however, colleges cover a fraction of their students' demonstrated financial need (COA minus EFC). Perhaps 50 percent or as much as 80 percent. A small number of well-endowed universities pride themselves on meeting 100 percent of their students' demonstrated financial need.[4] Regardless of the percentage, and higher is clearly better, you need to understand two things.

First, some of your demonstrated financial need might be "met" by the offer of a loan. But you can reject that part and accept just the grants, scholarships, and any work-study offer. That's your call. However, rejecting one type of financial aid will not lead to increases in other types of financial aid.

Second, colleges can offer to meet one student's $20,000 demonstrated financial need with $15,000 in scholarships and $5,000 in loans. And they can offer to meet a less desirable student's similar need with $5,000 in scholarships and $15,000 in loans. This is called preferential packaging. As I said in Trap 3, go to collegedata.com to compare *your* financial aid offer with how that college typically offers, on average, to meet the financial needs of its students. It's nice to know where you stack up. That information, along with offers from other colleges, might allow you to negotiate, respectfully, with your preferred college.

Private Scholarships Are Overrated

Every year we hear stories about "millions of dollars going unclaimed." You might hear that if you attend a special seminar, you'll learn secrets "guaranteed" to win you big money. Take these promises with a large grain of salt. And run away if someone asks you to pay money for the chance to win money. It's probably a scam.

Yes, private scholarship money exists, and you can easily spend several weeks doing nothing but filling out applications, but, as college admissions expert Lynn O'Shaughnessy points out, only 7 percent of college students receive a private scholarship, and the average award is $2,500.[5] To make matters worse, private scholarships usually only last for one year. The kicker is that any private scholarship funds you win tend to decrease your demonstrated financial need. For example, if you were going to receive an aid package of $15,000, and you win a $4,000 private scholarship, it reduces your aid package to $11,000. That's not a problem if you get to keep all the institutional scholarships and work-study funds your college was planning to throw your way. But that depends on your college's outside scholarship policy. At some schools, winning $4,000 in a private scholarship means losing $4,000 the school would have otherwise given you.

If you've got a solid lead on a private scholarship, and after some quick research you think you've got a decent shot, go for it. When I was a junior in college, a professor suggested I enter a writing contest for which only a few hundred students in the country were even eligible. Only about a dozen bothered to apply. I was one of the two winners who each snagged $5,000.

So it does happen. But killing yourself looking for

obscure contests is usually not worth the effort. If you're up for it, prioritize local or regional scholarships where your chances of winning are greater, thanks to fewer applicants. Check with your local library, high school guidance counselor, and your parents' workplaces. If you want to sample the universe of what's out there, popular websites include Fastweb.com and Scholarships.com.

But be clear on this: The vast majority of scholarship funds comes from colleges and universities themselves. And they *typically* are renewable each year, provided you still meet the eligibility requirements.

Grants: Need-Based Gifts

Grants are the best kind of need-based aid because they don't need to be repaid. The federal government offers two grants: the Federal Pell Grant and the Federal Supplemental Educational Opportunity Grant (FSEOG). The maximum Federal Pell Grant award for the 2014–2015 academic cycle is $5,730. To qualify for a Federal Pell Grant, your EFC must be less than 90 percent of the maximum Federal Pell Grant. The amount of your grant is roughly equal to the difference between the maximum grant and your EFC. Keep in mind that students from low-income families can have EFCs as low as zero. The Federal Supplemental Educational Opportunity Grant (FSEOG) is an annual award somewhere in the range of $100 and $4,000 (but usually, I'm told, for about $600 a year).

One difference between the Federal Pell Grant and the FSEOG is that whereas the Federal Pell Grant *guarantees* funds to every eligible student, schools receive a limited pool of FSEOG funds each year. Once the FSEOG funds are claimed, they're gone until the next year. Other college or university award money works similarly. So it's best to apply for college financial aid early in the financial aid application cycle.

Individual states also have need-based grants, such as the generous Cal Grant in California (up to $12,192 per year to pay for college expenses at any qualifying California college at the time of this writing). Some states offer discounted or free admission to a state university if you graduate near the top of your high school class. Similarly, some states offer grants based only on your family's income, not on their assets (such as your parents' nonretirement savings and investment accounts, which *are* considered by the FAFSA). Look into what's available in your state, as it could point to a lower-cost route through college, though it will probably mean needing to choose an in-state school. And don't just ask one person. Do your own research and consult several sources to verify what you find. Your state legislator's office, for example, should be able to point you to reliable information regarding state grants and incentives.

Work-Study: Need-Based Self-Help

Work-study awards of about $2,500 per year are not uncommon. Work-study funds are not free; they must be earned through a part-time, on-campus job related to your course of study or a part-time, off-campus job related to community service and the public good (such as a nonprofit organization). I'll say more about work-study jobs in Trap 6. One spoiler for now: What's nice about money you earn in a work-study job is that it helps cover your cost of attendance, *and* it does not raise your expected family contribution for the next year.

Loans: Need-Based Self-Help

The least desirable form of need-based aid is a loan. Unlike scholarships, grants, and work-study funds, loans must be repaid with interest over many years after you graduate. Since colleges routinely include loans in their financial aid packages, it's important that you understand how loans work. The *interest rate* of a loan determines how much additional money (interest) you have to pay back beyond what was borrowed (principal). Let's say a bank lends you $10,000 at a 10 percent interest rate and requires repayment in monthly increments over ten years. That works out to just $132.15 per month. No, I didn't figure that out in my head or on my calculator. I went to a loan amortization calculator (just Google "loan amortization calculator," and you'll find several good ones). *Amortization* is just a fancy word that refers to paying back what you owe by making regular payments over a defined period of time.

Paying $132.15 per month over ten years in exchange for getting $10,000 *right now* may seem like a good deal. But here's the downside: If you multiply $132.15 by 120 (the number of months in ten years), you'll find that you're actually paying back $15,858 over ten years. That's a lot more than $10,000! If your interest rate had been 5 percent, you'd be paying back only $12,728—a savings of about $3,000. That's the benefit of a low interest rate. The monthly payment for the loan with the 10 percent interest rate would only be about $25 higher than the loan with the 5 percent interest rate, but that small difference adds up to about $3,000 over ten years.

A *fixed* interest rate guarantees that your monthly payments won't increase. That's huge. A lot of people got in trouble a few years ago when they purchased homes with adjustable rate mortgages. These loans started off with really low interest rates, but then they adjusted upward, leaving families unable to make the larger monthly payments.

Federal loans have fixed interest rates, along with a few consumer protections that aren't available with private loans. For these reasons, colleges tend to refer students to federal loans first. The three kinds of federal loans are Federal Stafford loans, Federal Perkins loans, and Federal PLUS loans.

Federal Loans

Federal Stafford loans.[6] You take out a Federal Stafford loan for a given academic year at a specific fixed interest rate (4.66 percent for undergraduate students and 6.21 percent for graduate students in 2014–2015). Once you've taken out the loan, the interest rate *on that loan* cannot change. But if you take out *another* Federal Stafford loan the *next* academic year, it will probably have a different interest rate.[7] If you take out multiple loans, which is common for those who borrow, aim to anticipate your *total* monthly payment after graduation—and set an upper limit on that figure based on your future earnings prospects. We'll come back to this later.

Federal Stafford loans have maximum annual amounts, depending on your academic standing and your FAFSA dependency status (dependent or independent student). The latter has to do with your level of access to your parents' money. It's rare for undergraduate students to have independent status, even if they're paying their own way through college.[8]

Here are the annual Federal Stafford Loan limits:[9]

Annual Federal Stafford Loan Limits	Dependent	Independent
First Year	$5,500	$9,500
Second Year	$6,500	$10,500
Third Year and Beyond	$7,500	$12,500
Cumulative	$31,000	$57,500

Federal Stafford loans don't require a credit check or a cosigner. However, if you have financial need *as determined by the FAFSA*, part of your Federal Stafford loan can be *subsidized*. What does *subsidized* mean in this context? It means that as long as you're in school at least half-time and for a six-month grace period after you leave college, the government will pay the interest on your loan. If your entire Federal Stafford loan is subsidized, it's essentially an interest-free loan until six months after you graduate. But loans are subsidized only up to a lower set of annual thresholds: $3,500 (first year), $4,500 (second year), and $5,500 for subsequent years, with a cumulative limit of $23,000.[10] So a freshman might take out a $3,500 subsidized Federal Stafford loan and a $2,000 unsubsidized Federal Stafford loan, at which point he or she would hit the annual maximum for the Federal Stafford loan program.

Federal Stafford loans have a 1.072 percent origination fee. This fee is automatically deducted when the funds are disbursed—which, as is required for student loans, goes first to your college to cover tuition, fees, and room and board. Anything left over is refunded to you to fund your living costs. You may find that some college students use extra loan money to live it up, but that's a big mistake. By all means, take care of your essential food, housing, and textbook needs, but beyond that, you'd be wise to ask the college's financial aid office to return the excess money to the lender. There's no penalty for this, and in the case of unsubsidized loans, it lowers the total interest that accrues.

Federal Perkins loans. Colleges will offer you a Federal Perkins loan only if you qualify, which requires you to demonstrate exceptional financial need as determined by the FAFSA. Perkins loans have a fixed 5 percent interest rate, *no* origination fee, and a *nine-month* grace period after graduation during which interest does not accrue. Federal Perkins loans are also subsidized (the interest is paid by the government as long as you're in school at least half-time) and have better cancellation/forgiveness provisions than Federal Stafford loans.

Two words of caution: One, not all schools participate in the Federal Perkins loan program. For those that do, the *school*, not the U.S. Department of Education, is the lender. Two, due to limited funds, not everyone who qualifies for a Federal Perkins loan receives one. If you think you might qualify for a Federal Perkins loan, make sure the schools you're applying to participate in the program, submit your FAFSA as close to January 1 as possible, and apply for college financial aid early in the financial aid application cycle. The current maximum eligibility in the Perkins loan program is $5,500 per year for undergraduate students (with a cumulative maximum of $27,500).

Federal PLUS loans. A college may suggest a Federal PLUS loan to help meet your cost of attendance (COA), but Federal PLUS loans are for parents and graduate students only. To qualify for a Federal PLUS loan, the applicant must not have an adverse credit history, such as a recent foreclosure, defaulted loan, unpaid collection accounts, or bankruptcy discharge. Unlike Federal Stafford and Federal Perkins loans, Federal PLUS loans have no cumulative limit. Mom and Dad can borrow as much as they need to send you to a college of *any* cost for as many years as necessary, regardless of how much other debt they have, regardless of their annual income, and regardless of whether they're even employed![11] They're limited only by your college's cost of attendance (COA).

As I write, the interest rate for Federal PLUS loans is fixed at 7.21 percent, and there's a hefty onetime 4.282 percent origination fee. Like other federal loans, Federal PLUS loans offer virtually no bankruptcy protection. To make matters worse, Federal PLUS loans are generally *not* eligible for the income-based repayment plans I'll describe later in this chapter.

Frankly, I think Federal PLUS loans are a lousy deal. For one thing, why should your parents *borrow* money to send you to college? They're closer to retirement age than you are, so they're more in need of building their own savings in case they get sick or injured and need to stop working. For another, you can get up to $31,000 of Federal Stafford loans with a lower interest rate than your parents can access. Shouldn't that be enough? Finally, if your parents *are* going to borrow, they could probably do better by taking out some of the equity in their home. As I write, the interest rates on such arrangements are well below 7.21 percent.[12] And if your parents have little to no home equity or savings, then they are truly in no position to borrow money to pay for your college education!

Private Student Loans

Private student loans are the final option colleges will present to help a student cover his or her cost of attendance (COA). With private student loans the interest rates are often variable, not just over the life of the loan's repayment, but from student to student. That's because with private student loans your interest rate and your annual and cumulative loan limits depend on your credit history. In fact, more than 90 percent of new private student loans to undergraduate students require creditworthy cosigners. But the problem with having Mom and Dad cosign your loan is that it puts them on the hook for your debt. Some private loans are not dischargeable even in death, meaning you could pass away in a car accident or drop dead on the football field, and your mom and dad would have to pay back what you borrowed.

Sometimes the *advertised* interest rate on a private loan is the lender's preferred rate, available only for applicants with the best credit scores (the top 5 to 10 percent or so). Students with bad credit will have to pay considerably higher interest rates. And most students can expect their rates to increase throughout their repayment period, as the interest rate may "reset" monthly, quarterly, or annually as prevailing interest rates change.

I'm convinced private loans are unsafe and unwise for at least three reasons: First, their interest rates are often variable, which means your monthly payment can significantly increase once you enter repayment.[13] Second, there are even fewer loan forgiveness protections with private loans than with federal loans. For example, my friend Josh graduated with $90,000 in student debt. After a couple of years of working hard and struggling to make payments, he joined the military. After Josh puts in ten years of service, Uncle Sam will forgive all his *federal* student loan debt but not his private loan debt. Those loans he must repay in full. Third, it's hard to see why anyone should borrow more than the federal loan limits for an undergraduate education. Is a college that would require you to borrow more than $31,000 (or $58,500 if you also qualify for a Federal Perkins loan) *really* worth that kind of money? Aren't there other colleges you could attend that would be more affordable, and not much different in academic quality? Remember the pitfalls we discussed in Trap 3. The federal loan limits on Federal Stafford and Federal Perkins loans are there for a reason. Congress — not exactly known for fiscal responsibility — thought that was enough extra money to get you through.

How Normal Is Massive Student Debt?

It's easy to hear student debt horror stories and to normalize what's actually an atypical experience. This is dangerous because you're more likely to do what you think is normal, even if it means borrowing $20,000 per year for college. The truth is that about three in ten students earn a bachelor's degree with absolutely no debt. Zippo. In the class of 2012, half of the graduates walked the stage with less than $17,000 in debt. Not too bad. But among those in the class of 2012 who did borrow, their average debt load was almost $30,000. That sounds like a lot, right? But here's the thing: Only 10 percent of undergraduate borrowers in the class of 2012 had more than $49,000 in debt. Go into six figures (like Kelsey in Trap 3), and you're in the top 0.3 percent.[14]

So taking out more than $10,000 in each of the four or five years of your undergraduate program is not normal, no matter what anyone tells you. If that's what you've already done, don't give up. In Trap 9, we'll discuss strategies for getting free from even large amounts of debt.

I don't deny there are success stories among adults who've taken out loads of loans. Doctors and lawyers routinely take out more than $100,000 in debt for their undergraduate and graduate education (combined). But they have the potential to rake in hefty salaries, even early in their careers. So if you're pursuing a bachelor's degree, think twice before taking out a private student loan. Consider your likely starting salary and the many other expenses you'll face once you graduate. Minimizing debt during your undergraduate years will give you more options later in life. There *are* less expensive ways to make it through. (We'll talk about earning more and spending less during your college years in Traps 6 and 7.)

Before You Borrow! Calculate Your Future Monthly Payment

Earlier I explained how to calculate the monthly payment associated with a loan based on the loan's interest rate. Before you take out a single loan, let alone multiple loans, you want to know how much you'll owe each month after you graduate. And you want to compare this number to your probable future salary. How else will you know if you're likely to make ends meet or if you'll need to live in a cardboard box?

If your Federal Stafford loan is unsubsidized, or if a portion is unsubsidized, you have to pay the interest while you're in school or the interest will be rolled into the loan balance, on which you will have to start making payments six months after you graduate. Let's do a calculation on a $5,000 unsubsidized Federal Stafford loan taken at a 5 percent interest rate during your freshman year. First off, you'd pay a 1 percent origination fee to open the loan ($50). Then, the annual interest would be about $250 per year (5 percent of $5,000).

So if you graduated in four years and hadn't paid the interest while you were in school, you'd owe about $6,050 ($1,000 in interest, plus the origination fee).[15] That'll cost you about $65 per month for ten years. Again, I came up with this figure using a loan amortization calculator. I punched in $6,050 as my mortgage amount, a 5 percent interest rate, and a ten-year repayment period with monthly payments. I got $64.17 per month and then rounded to $65 to be safe.

According to Mark Kantrowitz, publisher of Edvisors.com, the monthly payment on a Federal Stafford loan with a ten-year repayment term is about 1 percent of the loan balance when the loan enters repayment. So just chop off the two least significant digits. In the example given above, that yields a monthly payment of about $61, not far off from the actual $64 monthly payment.

Take out a $5,000 Federal Stafford loan in *each* of your four years, and you're looking at a monthly tab of about $240 when you're done (on a balance of roughly $22,700).[16]

Which brings us to the question, How much debt is too much?

How Much Debt Is Too Much?

The answer to this question depends on your prospective salary after graduation, how likely you are to be employed at that salary, and what your living costs will be. Remember Emily, whose story I told in the introduction? She was earning $40,000 per year. But the costs associated with living on her own made a $250 monthly student loan payment seem like a big deal to her. Why? Where was all her money going? It was Emily's conviction that she give 10 percent back to God. Uncle Sam was taking about 27 percent in the form of federal and state income taxes, along with Social Security and Medicare contributions.[17] Most employees have additional funds withheld from their paychecks for health insurance and retirement, but even ignoring those, you get something like this:

Annual Salary	Annual Salary (After Tithe)	Annual Salary (After Taxes)	Monthly Take-Home Pay
$35,000	$31,500	$22,173	$1,848
$40,000	**$36,000**	**$25,340**	**$2,112**
$45,000	$40,500	$28,508	$2,376
$50,000	$45,000	$31,365	$2,640
$55,000	$49,500	$34,843	$2,904

The bold numbers in the chart above reflect Emily's situation. Her monthly loan bill of $250 represents a bit more than 10 percent of her take-home pay. To remember why this was a big deal, recall what her take-home pay needed to cover:

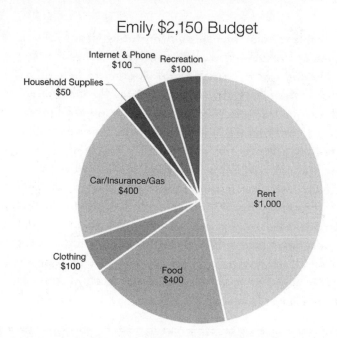

Emily $2,150 Budget

Emily didn't have any money left at the end of the month to cover her loan payment of $250 on a balance of $23,000. Can you see how she would have *really* been in trouble had she exceeded the $31,000 cap on Federal Stafford loans?

But what if you've already borrowed more than you can pay with a standard ten-year repayment plan? That's where alternative repayment plans come in handy.

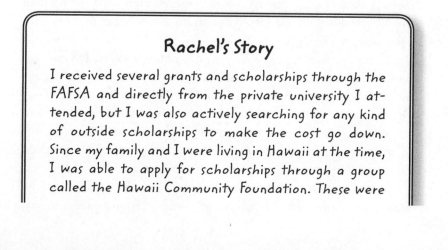

Rachel's Story

I received several grants and scholarships through the FAFSA and directly from the private university I attended, but I was also actively searching for any kind of outside scholarships to make the cost go down. Since my family and I were living in Hawaii at the time, I was able to apply for scholarships through a group called the Hawaii Community Foundation. These were renewable scholarships through my four years of school, as long as I resubmitted all the materials every April.

My dad was adamant about wanting to help all of us kids with college. He had paid his way through school and was drowning in student debt after he graduated. It was something he didn't want us to experience. I'm incredibly grateful for his generosity, and while I have some student debt, it's not as much as it could've been.

Now that I've finished school and started this new chapter of my life, it still feels like I'm caught in this weird in-between. My loan payments will start soon, and I'm nervous. I have a family assistant position that pays well and is helping me save money, but it's only guaranteed through the end of August. It's a constant stress as the month winds down.

Alternative Repayment Plans

The *Graduated Repayment Plan* begins with low monthly payments that increase every two years. Your monthly payments will never grow to more than three times the initial payment. The idea is that as you start earning more, you can presumably afford to make higher payments. The repayment period is still ten years.[18] This plan might work for someone who isn't earning much but expects to earn a lot more in a few years.

There are two types of *Extended Repayment Plans*. If you have more than $30,000 in federal loans, the first kind of extended repayment plan allows you to make lower payments over a twenty-five-year period without consolidating your loans. If you have less than $30,000 in federal loans, you can consolidate (combine) your loans in order to get a longer repayment plan. Your repayment term would be ten to thirty years, depending on your debt level.[19]

If your monthly payment under the standard (ten-year) repayment plan is more than 15 percent of your discretionary income, you may qualify for the *Income-Based Repayment (IBR) Plan*. Your discretionary income is defined as the difference between your adjusted gross income and 150 percent of the poverty level (which is about $11,500 for a single adult). Under IBR, your monthly payment is set at 15 percent of your discretionary income.

For example, Emily's annual salary was $40,000. One hundred fifty percent of the poverty level for her is $17,250. That puts her discretionary income at $22,750 per year or $1,895 per month. Her monthly payment under the Standard Repayment Plan is $250, about 13 percent of her discretionary income. Emily would *not* qualify for the IBR Plan.

But what if Emily had $40,000 in debt? Now her monthly payment, under the standard ten-year repayment plan, would be about $425 (assuming a 5 percent interest rate), which is slightly more than 22 percent of her discretionary income. Now she might qualify for IBR, which would lower her monthly payment to $284 (15 percent of $1,895), a reduction of about $150 per month.[20]

An upside of the IBR plan is that after twenty-five years the remaining balance is usually forgiven. In fact, if you're employed full-time for a public service organization, such as a public school, library, police, or the military, the remainder is forgiven after just ten years.[21] Downsides of the IBR plan are (1) you have to submit annual documentation; (2) you'll usually wind up paying more interest because you're making payments for a longer period of time (see sidebar "Estimating Your Monthly Loan Payment"); and (3) you may have to pay taxes on any loan forgiveness you receive.

Don't forget: These alternative repayment plans are only available with *federal* student loan programs. If you want a flexible repayment plan with a private student loan, you're at the mercy of your lender. That's another reason to avoid private loans. Finally, neither federal nor private loans can be discharged in bankruptcy (which I'll discuss a bit later in this chapter).

Some people who qualify for IBR also qualify for a newer, more generous plan called *Pay as You Earn Repayment (PAYER)*. This plan requires you to pay only 10 percent of your discretionary income instead of 15 percent. The remaining balance is forgiven after

Estimating Your Monthly Loan Payment

Student Loan Balance at Graduation	Monthly Payment (10-Year Repayment)	Total Interest Paid
$10,000	$106	$2,728
$20,000	$212	$5,456
$30,000	$318	$8,184
$40,000	$424	$10,911

Student Loan Balance at Graduation	Monthly Payment (25-Year Repayment)	Total Interest Paid
$10,000	$58	$7,538
$20,000	$117	$15,075
$30,000	$175	$22,613
$40,000	$234	$30,151

For simplicity, a 5 percent fixed interest rate is assumed throughout. Note that you can drastically lower your monthly payments with a twenty-five-year repayment plan, but you end up *spending about three times as much on interest over the repayment period.* Money paid against the *principal* knocks down your loan balance. Money paid against the *interest* is a loss — a cost associated with borrowing money.

twenty years in repayment instead of twenty-five years of payments. Borrowers must have at least one loan disbursed on or after October 1, 2011, and no loans from prior to October 1, 2007, to qualify for PAYER. These restrictions may change.

You'll often hear "don't borrow more than your annual salary." I'd like to see you borrow considerably less. Emily's story illustrates why. If Emily had $40,000 in debt, her monthly payment would have been more than $400. Unless she was an independent student (rare) or qualified for a Perkins loan (also uncommon), that would mean she took out private loans during her undergraduate years (not wise). Perhaps she'd be able to lower her monthly payments by qualifying for Income-Based Repayment (IBR) or Pay as You Earn Repayment (PAYER). But either plan would mean making loan payments until she's in her mid- to late-forties. Not fun. And it might ultimately cost her a lot more in terms of interest payments. For these reasons, I suggest a few safer guidelines: Don't borrow more than *half* your anticipated salary; stay below the cumulative limit on Federal Stafford loans; and avoid private loans.

Deferment and Forbearance

Now let's talk about your options if you can't make your payments in full each month. The first strategy is to pursue one of the alternative repayment plans we discussed earlier, particularly IBR or PAYER, which were designed to help graduates with low incomes. If you don't qualify for IBR or PAYER, or you do qualify but still can't find a way to make your monthly payments, deferment and forbearance become considerations.

Deferment on federal loans is an entitlement for which you qualify if you meet certain conditions. If you're enrolled at least half-time in a college or career school (including graduate school), unemployed, or experiencing economic hardship (defined as having an annual income less than 150 percent of the poverty line applicable to your family size), there's a good chance you can get a deferment.

If you meet the qualifications for a deferment, you can submit a request to your loan servicer. If you're enrolled in a college or career school, you should also contact your institution's financial aid office. The deferment lasts until you graduate or are no longer enrolled at least half-time. In the case of unemployment or economic hardship, deferment is up to three years.[22]

Here's what happens in deferment: The federal government pays the interest on any Federal Perkins loans and subsidized Federal Stafford loans. The federal government does *not* pay the interest on your unsubsidized loans. You don't have to make loan payments during deferment, but the interest does continue to accumulate on unsubsidized loans. Many people fail to recognize this and then wonder why their balance when they enter deferment is higher than the amount they borrowed. That's what will happen unless you pay the interest on an unsubsidized loan.

If you're not entitled to deferment, the last option is *forbearance*. Forbearance on a federal loan is usually at the discretion of the lender but is mandatory in some (rare) cases.[23] On a private loan, forbearance is always at the discretion of the lender. As with deferment, in forbearance you don't have to make loan payments, but interest continues to accumulate. But unlike deferment, the federal government does *not* pay the interest on *any* type of loan during a forbearance, not even on subsidized loans.

Delinquency and Default

Your loan becomes delinquent the day after you are late with a payment. It remains delinquent until you make all the payments you've missed, at which point your loan is said to be "current" (up-to-date). Even a thirty-day delinquency is sufficient to reduce your credit score. Since potential landlords and employers often check credit scores, this can really hurt you.

If you don't make your loan payments for 360 days, your loan enters *default*. Then what? Your entire unpaid loan balance (including any interest and late fees that have accrued) becomes due immediately. You lose eligibility for deferment, forbearance, and the various alternative repayment plans I mentioned earlier. Your loan account gets assigned to a collection agency, whose job it is to contact you and encourage you to start making payments. If you're employed, your wages might be garnished. If you have a tax refund, it can be snatched and applied to your debt. In short, life gets ugly.

Maybe you're thinking, *Yeah, but it could never happen to me.* What if I told you that one in four borrowers who entered repayment in 2005 had become delinquent on their loans at some point before 2010 and that one in seven had gone into default?[24] Combined, just over 40 percent of these borrowers struggled with delinquency or default in the five-year span ranging from 2005 to 2010. Similar default rates have more recently been reported for just a three-year span (2009–2012).[25]

Students from for-profit schools tend to struggle the most. Although these schools enroll just 13 percent of students nationwide, their students represent 46 percent of those who default on their student loans.[26] The problem is twofold: (1) For-profit schools tend to be more expensive, and (2) they tend to attract students from lower-income backgrounds. But lots of students from nonprofit colleges, both private and public, borrow and struggle to make repayment. It's not just the amount borrowed. It's asking the right questions before you borrow. And it's having the discipline and the means to pay back what you've borrowed.

The Bottom Line

Student loans are *not* always worth it, because college is not worth it at any price. College makes sense for the right students at the right price. But someone else's right price may not be your right price. You don't have a constitutional right to a $50,000 per year education. Ask yourself, If I get a great education but come out with crippling debt, is that a deal I can live with? If not, why not attend a less expensive college (see Trap 3)? Besides, getting a great education usually has more to do with the passion and love of learning that you bring to the classroom than it does with the resources of the school. Consider the checklist for getting a degree without going broke (it's located at the front of the book). And with that, let's shift our attention to two other factors that play a big role in beating the college debt trap: earning more and spending less during your college years.

PART 3

TAKING CHARGE
EARNING AND MANAGING YOUR MONEY

TRAP 6

I CAN'T GET MEANINGFUL WORK AS A STUDENT

Be creative and resourceful —
you'll set yourself up for long-term success

Let's start with the obvious: Fewer and fewer parents believe they can help their children pay for college.[1] Even if Mom and Dad are helping, there's a good chance you're planning to work part-time while going to school. That's great, but it's not enough. You want to be strategic in order to maximize the work part of your life. Beating the college debt trap requires taking the bull by the horns, thinking differently, and living strategically. You don't just want to accept any odd job that comes along. Now's the time to pursue meaningful work — the kind that pays good money and/or allows you to develop the skills and track record that will command the attention of future employers. Setting yourself up for long-term success begins today. This chapter will give concrete ideas about how you can pay for college, leverage your current skills, develop new capacities, and build a network of strategic relationships — all before graduation.

First, let's consider how many hours you should work when classes are in session.

How Much Should You Work?

There's a real danger of overtaxing yourself, especially if you're maxed out on classes. Many colleges charge the same tuition for a student who takes anywhere between twelve and eighteen semester units.[2] To speed things up and because it makes good financial sense, students load up their schedule to eighteen units. And then they also land a twenty-five to thirty hours per week off-campus job and wonder why they never have time to study. This is becoming a bigger problem as college expenses go up and students feel increasingly squeezed. What to do?

I used to take the view that since being a full-time student was a full-time job, full-time students should not seek another job while classes are in session. As a professor, I have a bias for wanting my students' undivided attention. The historical rule of thumb for studying is "two hours out of class for every one hour in class," which means that if you're taking fifteen semester units, you should be studying thirty hours per week. That's a forty-five hour per week commitment.

But as I said in Trap 4, study times these days are closer to twelve hours per week. Even in 1961, full-time college students studied twenty-four hours per week, not thirty hours.[3] While I'm concerned that students who put little into their education are unlikely to get much out of it, the flip side is that it's probably unrealistic to expect today's students to live in their books for thirty hours per week. Unless you're in an especially demanding major, you probably don't need to study that hard to do well; at some point there are diminishing returns to extra studying, and—most importantly—there are essential skills and habits that can only be learned on the job, especially co-op/internship-type jobs (see below).

So how much is too much to work when classes are in session? Start with ten to fifteen hours per week and see how you're able to handle your coursework. Make a schedule, but also monitor how you *actually* spend your time. You might be embarrassed by how many hours you waste surfing the Internet or keeping up with your friends on Instagram, Facebook, and other social media platforms. A lot of college students spend more time socializing and relaxing than they do studying and working. If you're fulfilling all your work-study hours (more about this later) and doing well in your classes, and you've got extra time, look for more work. Prioritize jobs that allow you to develop professional skills or make connections with people who can help you later. If you're a journalism or graphic arts major, could you get paid to learn web design or photography? If you're a math major, could you get a job tutoring at a nearby high school or elsewhere in the community? These kinds of jobs have two benefits: the money you make now, and the skills and relationships you develop for the future.

But before you start looking for a job, let me explain why you should fulfill work-study hours first. It has to do with the funky Expected Family Contribution (EFC) formula used by the FAFSA.

The More You Earn, the More Colleges Expect You to Pay

You fill out the FAFSA every year. It spits out an Expected Family Contribution (EFC). If either you or your family get richer, your college expects you to pay more. What many don't know is that the formula used to calculate a student's EFC weights *your* earnings much higher than those of your parents. I'll make it simple: You're allowed to earn $6,310 pretax dollars.[4] *Any extra earning raises your EFC by 50 cents for every additional dollar you make.* Let's say you earn $9,310 pretax dollars, $3,000 more than the cutoff. Your EFC will go up by $1,500.

It gets worse. Let's say you pocket the remaining $1,500 in your checking account. You're saving up to buy a car, but you don't yet have enough cash. That money now qualifies as an asset and is taxed by FAFSA at a 20 percent rate.[5] So your EFC rises by another $300. That's right—you work hard and earn an extra $3,000, and whatever college you're attending expects $1,800 of it. A whopping 70 percent effective tax rate.[6]

> **The money you earn in a work-study job won't raise your EFC by one penny.**

But there's a loophole you won't want to miss: The money you earn in a work-study job won't raise your EFC by one penny.

Work-Study Jobs

As I briefly mentioned in our discussion of Trap 5, work-study funds must be earned through a part-time, on-campus job related to your course of study or a part-time, off-campus job related to community service and the public good (such as a nonprofit organization). Most work-study awards allow for between ten and twenty hours of work per week at a salary close to minimum wage. Unfortunately, many students don't work all the hours they're assigned. That's almost always a mistake because you'd have to make a lot more money off campus to make it worth giving up money that's shielded from the EFC formula. Think about it: If you make $20 per hour off campus, but your college takes half of it, it's as if you're earning $10 per hour. Why not first fulfill all your work-study hours and *then* put in some off-campus hours if you have the extra time?

You might be thinking: *Yeah, but work-study jobs are ridiculous. I don't want to wash dishes in the cafeteria.* If you inquire at your college, and do so early, you might be surprised at the variety of work-study jobs available. Are there options that would let you develop your professional skills and earn a strong letter of recommendation? Could you be a tutor for courses in which you did well? Could you work in the library digging up original sources for a history prof? If you're tech savvy, could you work in IT support? If you're a science or an engineering major, could you be a teaching assistant in a course with a laboratory component? Regardless of your major, could you get a meaningful community service assignment through which you can make a difference in the lives of others while expanding your horizons? At smaller schools, outstanding undergraduates are sometimes hired to perform tasks reserved for graduate students at larger universities. Be creative and proactive. Approach professors you like — especially if you've done well in their classes — and ask if they know of any available positions.

If only monotonous work-study options are available, look for ones that let you study on the job. If you're paid minimum wage but can study half the time, it's as if they're paying you twice the salary. Bonus: If you live on campus, you won't have to drive to work (losing time and gas money), and remember, your earnings don't raise your EFC by one penny.

Work-study jobs are strategic for the money and convenience and, if you play it right, for the skill development and networking. But internships and co-op jobs are usually even more strategic.

Internships & Co-op Programs

Internships and co-op programs represent two forms of what's known as experiential education. Learning by doing has become ultra-important in today's job market. Students who participate in these programs and perform well have vastly higher chances of securing high-paying, full-time employment after college. That alone is reason to pursue them, even if the paycheck is small or nonexistent.

The terms *co-op* and *internship* are sometimes used interchangeably, but they carry different meanings. *Co-op* stands for Cooperative Education. It's a joint venture between **As of July 2010, all money earned through co-ops is excluded from the FAFSA formula that determines EFC, just like money earned from work-study jobs.** your school, a particular employer, and you. Typically, there are two or three work terms, usually semesters, alternating with school terms. If the work is full-time, you're out of school for that semester. If the work is part-time, it will probably be about twenty hours per week over a total of three or more semesters during which you'll also be taking classes. Either way, you'll get paid and receive substantial training. You might rotate duties—for example, one semester in manufacturing, another in the business office, and so on.

Colleges and universities that have co-op programs usually include that information in their advertisements, and for good reason. Graduates from co-op programs are highly employable, and they can be given more responsibility on Day 1.

As of July 2010, there's one more reason co-ops are better than internships: All money earned through co-ops is excluded from the FAFSA formula that determines EFC (just like money earned from work-study jobs). Caveat: Attending a university that has a co-op program does not guarantee you'll personally participate. You'll want to inquire about the selection process and related criteria.

Internships are more common than co-ops. An internship is a onetime work assignment, often during a summer, in a specific area, such as marketing, human resources, production, or research and development. Positions can be full-time or part-time and paid or unpaid, depending on the organization. An internship doesn't interfere with your coursework, and participating students receive less training than they would in a co-op program.

Even if you lose some financial aid, internships are worth it for the experience, skill development, and networking. While it's easier to land an internship as a junior or senior, it's not impossible to get one earlier. My first internship came between my freshman and sophomore years. I got many rejections that year, but I only needed one group to say yes. I was a research assistant at Northwestern University in Evanston, Illinois, through the National Science Foundation's Research Experience for Undergraduates (REU) program. My duties included finding articles in the library, performing basic measurements in labs, and making a presentation at the end of the summer. Along the way, I received exposure to concepts that would come up in future coursework, giving me a huge advantage. And having an academic-related job on my résumé opened doors for other engineering/science-related jobs in future summers.

Leveraging Your Current Skills

Another option for meaningful, high-paying work is to leverage your existing skills. In her college days, my wife earned $20 per hour (in the 1990s) by teaching piano lessons to children. I earned almost as much tutoring math and physics. Other college students have started businesses—painting, doing yard work, moving furniture—and even hired their own employees. Looks pretty good on your résumé to say you started and managed your own business, particularly if it's one you can sell to another go-getter when you graduate.

The harder something is to do, or the less other people want to do it, the more they'll generally pay you if you can do it and do it well.

Last time I called a plumber, I paid $100 for a forty-five-minute visit. How could he charge so much? Because I was willing to pay it. When you need a plumber, it's often fairly urgent. You're calling because you can't or don't want to figure it out yourself. Which brings me back to what I said in Trap 1 about the value of skilled labor — fixing cars, doing electrical work, maintaining swimming pools, and so on. Part-time jobs in these areas can be quite lucrative. Private tutoring, teaching kids how to swim, or giving piano or violin lessons — same thing. These skills can support you during college far better than minimum-wage jobs, allowing you to minimize or avoid debt.

The tips you earn in customer service jobs in restaurants can add to your earnings, but retail sales jobs that supplement an hourly salary with commission have the potential to increase your income even more. For example, Verizon and AT&T often hire cell phone enthusiasts to secure new customers, either in their stores or at kiosks in the mall. I've heard of students going solo, flipping phones or other products on the secondary market using Craigslist and eBay. Any kind of sales experience has another advantage: It stands out on a résumé. It says not just that you're a good communicator, but that you're willing to take initiative, that you're results-oriented. These are some of the key attributes employers are looking for in new graduates.

It's also the case that selling yourself is something many of us are doing not just when we graduate but throughout our careers. More people than ever are keeping an updated résumé, collecting recommendations and endorsements on networks like LinkedIn and drumming up potential future business through contacts both old and new. It's a function of an economy where interconnectedness is high, job security is low, and outsourcing and freelancing have never been easier. So never discount the relationships you form through whatever work you do. My friend Nathan is a health care manager who produces music for television shows on the side. David is a graphic artist I know who lives in Hollywood and writes screenplays as a freelancer.

Perhaps you're wondering, *But if I make a ton of cash, didn't you say my EFC would go through the roof?* Four quick caveats to keep in mind:

1. Remember that your first $6,310 pretax dollars aren't factored into your EFC.
2. Even on what you earn beyond $6,310, your EFC won't go up as much as your income—so more income is still good. My point earlier was that it makes financial sense to first fulfill your work-study and/or co-op hours.
3. It's not just about the money you make; it's about how the work experience prepares you to access the job market after graduation.
4. For those of you attending public universities—which is how most students get through—your EFC is less of an issue because the *full* price has already been knocked down for *all students* (courtesy of the taxpayers). You don't have to worry about your EFC if you're not dependent on a particular college's generosity. The flip side is that the price tag of a public school can shoot up quickly if your state legislature and governor so choose.

Straight A's don't make up for a lack of work experience.

My second and third caveats speak to another reason I've become a big believer in students holding jobs during college: Working now prepares you for working later. Trust me, straight A's don't make up for a lack of work experience.

Working Now Prepares You for Working Later

Attitude counts. Entrepreneur and anti-debt guru Dave Ramsey said it well, so I won't try to improve on it: "If you tell me you worked three part-time jobs to get yourself through college, that is as impressive as the fact that you have the college degree, because I know not only are you smart, but you know how to work. If you walk into my office and go, 'I've got six degrees and seven million dollars in student loans and I've never worked a day in my life,' I'm not interested."[7] It's an exaggerated comparison, of course, but it makes the point well. A work ethic that's been demonstrated over several years by effort, resourcefulness, and perseverance speaks volumes.

As I mentioned in Trap 4, employers today are concerned that recent graduates lack professionalism, intrinsic motivation, and empathy—a lot of which comes down to simply following the Golden Rule ("do to others what you would have them do to you," Matthew 7:12). But widespread negative perceptions give you the chance to shatter the stereotypes and stand out from the pack. Whatever job you have, do it with all your heart, as if doing it for God himself (see Colossians 3:23). Truly take on the mind-set of a servant. Don't ever be too good for the job you have. If you don't like mopping floors and can get a more interesting job, fine. But until that happens, aim to become the best floor mopper on the planet. Give your full concentration to what seems like a mindless task, and work as hard and as smart as you can. Be a learner in whatever you're doing. Look for ways to improve, to do better work, and to accomplish more for your employer in less time.

Your job is to make your organization more successful. Give your employer a return on investment for having hired you. Don't expect instant feedback and continuous praise. Instead, persevere and add value. By looking out for these things, it will ultimately go better for you. When others, like your boss, are successful, they'll know your work helped make it happen. Raises, promotions, letters of recommendation, and new opportunities are the natural by-products.

Brandon's Story

During my junior and senior years in college, I was selected to work as a teaching assistant for the laboratory components of General Biology and Anatomy and Physiology. These TA positions paid well, but their true value came in strengthening my applications to medical schools, as was explicitly mentioned by each person who interviewed me in the process. Though unpaid, my summer internship in Maternal and Child Health at a clinic in rural Kenya played a pivotal role in solidifying my desire to become a physician.

In Kenya, I was exposed to diseases and health conditions that most people in the United States have never seen before. While there was appropriate oversight, I was given a level of responsibility in the care of my patients that I could not have received in the U.S. as an undergraduate student. Not only did this internship help me get accepted into several excellent medical schools; it also fanned the flame of my desire to practice medicine in the service of the poor for the glory of God.

Professionalism counts. Let me say a bit more about the kind of professionalism it will require to secure, keep, and succeed in the kinds of jobs I've been describing. First, be early or on time for any job-related appointment. First impressions count. Whether you're punching a clock or meeting someone for an interview, be punctual and dependable. Second, look the part. Come to the interview or the job well dressed, clean, and tidy. Fair or unfair, how you look says something about who you are. Third, practice appropriate e-mail etiquette. This is a big one. When you're looking for a job or relating to others on the job, e-mail is still the standard method of communication. *Don't text a coworker, boss, or professor without previously receiving permission to do so.*

And here are two quick tips for better e-mail communication:

1. *Include a specific, succinct subject.* The subject invites the other person to open the note. It also helps him or her locate the note later. The subject should be appropriately descriptive. I can't tell you how many e-mails I've received from students with no subject. If they're in my class that semester, then it's my job to read these e-mails and respond. But if I don't know the person or if I had him or her as a student three years ago? I'm afraid such e-mails often go

unopened and are soon forgotten. If there's more than one cycle of correspondence and your second message is about something else, revise the subject line on the e-mail. That way, each e-mail's subject is specific to the content of that note and makes it much easier to find later.

2. *Don't be too informal.* The person you're writing to isn't your best friend. And you're not texting or IMing them. Greet people appropriately, stating their last names if they're much older or hold higher ranks than you. "Hi" or even "Dear" (for a much older person) is better than "Hey." Use proper capitalization and punctuation, and take it easy on the excla-mation points!!! Lay off the emoticons, and avoid acronyms like lol, idk, and ttyl. A friendly tone is good, but not at the expense of professionalism. And don't mark your notes as urgent unless the information you're conveying is urgent *to the recipient.* The fact that your e-mail has a résumé attached or is inquiring about a job you really need does not make it urgent to the other person. And use spell-check! Nothing says careless and uneducated like typos and poor spelling.

Examples of Great College Jobs

We've talked about work-study positions, internships, and co-ops. I've mentioned the value of being a research assistant, a teaching assistant, or a tutor. And we've discussed the importance of attitude and professionalism. Now let me give you a few examples of other jobs that can help you earn cash, gain real-world experience, and develop marketable skills that are transferable to a wide variety of potential careers.

1. Resident assistant. An RA job screams "trustworthy, mature, leader, responsible, good communicator, with good people skills." Granted, the work of an RA is unpredictable. Issues can pop up late at night that affect your ability to study or to get a good night's sleep before having to take a test the next day. But if you're going to live on campus anyway, it's usually a great way to get free housing, not to mention the extra privacy of a single room.

2. IT support tech. Installing and troubleshooting computers and software can be a lifelong money-making hobby, if not an outright career if you do it well and enjoy it. But apart from that, it's a great way to demonstrate service orientation, professionalism, and a can-do work ethic. You'll make measurable contributions in the lives of those whose machines you restore or maintain. You'll sometimes work under the stress of a deadline or a frustrated client—truly a real-world experience. Your participation in a knowledge-based, task-oriented team environment will stand out to future employers.

Leverage the Internet

Why not, *right now,* leverage the Internet to find your voice, earn credibility, and make a difference? For example, start a blog or Twitter account that highlights the latest ideas and innovations in whatever field you're interested in—marketing, European history, presidential politics, American literature, or whatever. You don't have to be an expert to start. You just have to care. Start by linking to, summarizing, and interacting with the leading voices. Your comments can be part personal reflection, part professional assessment.

Review what you're reading for school or personal enrichment on websites like Amazon and Goodreads. You'll learn a ton and become a better thinker and writer. Cross-post the content on your blog and link to it from your Twitter account. As your work gets better, you'll soon have followers who won't care that you're still a student.

This issue of finding your voice is particularly important for creatives like writers, artists, and musicians. Maybe it's YouTube, iTunes, or Etsy instead of a blog. The point is you need a way to practice your craft and solicit feedback, to learn what works and what doesn't.

Obscurity can be a gift; it gives you the freedom to try, mess up, and get better. The fact that few students do this is all the more reason you should. An online presence is a great way to build a platform, connect with others who share your interests, and even find work opportunities down the road.

3. Campus tour guide. Colleges and universities are selective when it comes to hiring tour guides because there's a recruiting component involved. You need to be a good communicator, cheerful, energetic, professional in appearance, and an all-around model representative of your school. Experience as a campus tour guide is excellent if you want to get into sales, teaching, or anything that requires public speaking or customer service.

4. Institutional research assistant. Just about every college has an office of institutional research that crunches numbers incessantly. Whether it's summarizing results from course evaluations, assisting with program reviews, collecting assessment data for accreditors, and more, institutional research is increasingly important in the world of higher education. Other groups on campus examine freshman-to-sophomore retention rates, graduation rates, how minority students are doing, what percentage of students apply for financial aid and how many get it, and much more. If you enjoy numbers and charts and might want to get into management or consulting someday, an appointment in one of these areas could be a great fit.

5. Career center or alumni relations assistant. These jobs are great for networking. Working in the career center can expose you to opportunities you wouldn't otherwise hear about, with companies you may not have known existed. And alumni *love* talking to current students. Alumni played a crucial role in the jobs I got my sophomore year summer (at Oak Ridge National Laboratory), my junior year summer (at Motorola), and my first full-time job right out of college (at IBM). In each case, I was either hired or referred by an alumnus. If you're interested in event planning, advising, or mentoring students in their career pursuits, assisting in the campus career center or alumni relations office can be a great start.

By the way, the vast majority of college students fail to utilize the career service resources of their college.[8] Don't be among them. Before dismissing it or complaining about it, make sure you at least find out what your college's career center has to offer. The career center for my undergraduate engineering program, which had some five hundred students, consisted of just one go-getter woman and her assistant. Sandy worked hard, was responsive, and used to make her office available so students like me could conduct phone interviews. She was instrumental in my securing several internships and a full-time job. Whatever setup your school has, make sure you get the most from it.

6. *A variety of leadership positions.* When my wife was a college student, she was given the opportunity to run the linen service for the approximately sixteen hundred incoming freshmen. The goal was to deliver the linens to dorm rooms in advance *and* include the school logo on the products. She sourced the products (including labeling), advertised the service, received credit card orders, hired and paid others to sort the linens, and delivered all the items using a master key she convinced the school to lend her. After that, she ran a student store that competed nicely with the professionally run university bookstore. These experiences landed her in a leadership development program for a Fortune 500 company.

It's undeniable: Employers want to hire leaders because leaders make things happen. If you can earn money while developing genuine leadership experience in college, do it.

7. *Student brand manager.* Many large companies, including Chipotle, Coca-Cola, and General Mills, hire outgoing, popular students as brand managers or campus ambassadors. They see such students as valuable links to a new generation of potential customers. The job is to generate buzz for what the company offers (tacos, soda pop, and yes, even Cheerios) and to strengthen the brand or image of that company with other students on your campus and beyond. These jobs usually run fall and spring, with flexible hours, a guaranteed paycheck, free products (burritos, anyone?), and the occasional

performance bonus. You'll learn a ton about marketing, the power of social media, sales, and thinking outside the box. And of course, doing good work as a brand manager gets you an inside track on a company's summer internship and full-time job openings.

8. Arts and crafts online seller. The Internet and social media have made it easier for budding artists to start side businesses selling their products. If you have a passion for pottery, painting, jewelry, or any kind of handmade craft, you can open a shop on Etsy.com for free and start making money immediately. In 2013, more than a billion dollars in creative goods were exchanged. While few artists are hitting the jackpot, lots of people are drawing a side income by doing this. In the process, you'll learn a lot about entrepreneurship, sales, and marketing.[9]

Can Your Earnings Make a Difference?

Okay, so how much money can you make during college, and can it really make a difference? Let's crunch some numbers and take a look. Let's say you have ten hours per week of work-study over two fifteen-week semesters, at $10 per hour. Let's say you can get an additional five hours of work per week leveraging one of your skills, earning $15 per hour over thirty weeks (two semesters). Depending on your skill, you may be able to command even higher pay, but we'll be conservative. And let's say you can work fifty hours per week for fifteen additional weeks in the summer at $13 per hour. Sure, that's more than full-time, but, hey, you're young and healthy. If classes aren't in session, why not earn some extra cash if it'll help you minimize debt? This schedule still gives you seven weeks off per year for final exams and vacations. Here's what you'd make:

Work-Study	$3,000
Skill-Based Job	$2,250
Summer Job	$9,750
Total	**$15,000**

How far will that get you? Financial aid packages are all over the map at private universities, so let's use the College Board's average price tag for tuition and fees in 2014–2015 for an in-state student at a public, four-year university: $9,139.[10] That's assuming your tuition isn't lowered by grants or scholarships. Room and board runs another $9,804, according to the College Board. That comes to just under $19,000, about $4,000 more than the $15,000 you could earn. If your parents can cough up $4,000 (they'd get back $2,500 through the American Opportunity Tax Credit), you're basically there. You'd also get there if you qualified for an equivalent amount of state or federal grant aid, or if you applied any savings you accumulated while living at home and attending a less expensive community college.

The Bottom Line

You are the manager of your own brand, and it starts now. Don't just earn money in college; be strategic. Make good money *and* do meaningful work. Cultivate a humble yet positive, can-do attitude and display professionalism. Develop marketable skills and establish rapport with people who can help you later. Your jobs in school should pave the way for future opportunities. It won't be easy, but it really is possible to earn enough money to cover the majority of your college expenses *while* you're in school. Doing so will go a long way toward helping you beat the college debt trap.

TRAP 7

I CAN'T CONTROL MY EXPENSES

If you don't, who will?

Confession: I didn't have a budget in college. Nor did any of my friends. We weren't living high on the hog. We had meal plans and lived in a small college town. There wasn't much to do besides the cheap entertainment offered on campus.

But times have changed. Colleges are now quoting annual figures of $1,200 to 2,000 for *textbooks*. Campus housing runs $5,000 or more per year (*with* a roommate), and a meal plan will cost you another $5,000—about $10 per meal—not to mention what you might spend on other food. Then there are the usual fees on top of tuition.

Beating the college debt trap means knowing where your money is going and looking for creative ways to cut costs. It doesn't matter what other students are doing. *You* need to control your expenses. As in today. We're talking about a vital life skill. You need to live within your means so you have the means to live.[1] It isn't always fun, but it beats drowning in bills or getting chased by debt collectors. You need to live somewhere, but can you shave $200 per month

> **Beating the college debt trap means knowing where your money is going and looking for creative ways to cut costs. You need to live within your means so you have the means to live.**

by living off-campus or getting an extra roommate? You need to eat, but can you cut $75 per month with a smaller meal plan? You need materials for class, but how much can you save by leveraging the library, friends, rental services, and the used book market?

In this chapter, we'll work our way through the most common expense categories, with an eye toward cutting costs. Then we'll discuss the importance of a budget and why credit cards are overrated.

Housing

What you *need* is a room with a bed, a desk, a closet, and access to a bathroom. If you're going to college in your hometown, the natural way to save money is to live at home and commute. That's what the majority of students are doing.[2] Plus, unless you want to escape family drama, why live on-campus in a shared room when you can stay at home and perhaps even have your own room? Sure, you'll burn gas driving to and from campus, and the time spent commuting adds on to your day, but you'll probably save a few thousand dollars each year on housing.

Of course, living on-campus is more convenient and fun; it's a great way to make lots of friends and get involved. It's easier to get to class, access professors, and meet up with people to study or socialize. Some schools require freshmen and sophomores to live on-campus. The rationale is that you're more likely to successfully transition to the responsibilities of college if you don't also have to shop, cook, pay the bills, and manage roommate issues without the guidance of resident assistants. And you're more likely to get academic or personal help if you're living on-campus, both of which tend to keep students on the road to graduation.

But the price of college housing, like tuition, has been rising faster than inflation, and for similar reasons. You're paying for convenience. In some cases, you're paying for luxury, as a growing number of universities are competing to impress you with upscale rooms, fancy amenities, and housing that feels more like a resort than a dorm. Even if your college's housing isn't all that snazzy, you can probably save money by living off-campus *if* you can find some good roommates and are willing to put up with the extra hassle.

The Pros of On- and Off-Campus Living

On-Campus	Off-Campus
Convenient — walk or bike to classes, make new friends, find study groups, access professors and group study sessions	Can save money and get away from the late-night noise of university housing
Help from resident assistants for resolving roommate issues, if needed	Learn independence, conflict-resolution skills, budgeting skills (choose where to spend; see where your money goes)
Can leave for the summer without needing to find a subletter	Not required to leave housing when classes are out of session

If you live on-campus, you don't have to worry about breaking a lease to go home (or wherever) for the summer. But most colleges have an annoying habit of kicking you out during some of the academic breaks, unless you can justify why you should be allowed to stay. When you do the math, you're only getting, at most, eight months of housing over two semesters or three quarters.[3] (Summer housing may be an option, but it'll cost extra.)

If you live off-campus, most landlords will want to stick you with a twelve-month lease. If you go home for the summer, finding a subletter will be your responsibility. You can ask for a nine-month lease, but most landlords will make you pay extra to get one. Summer classes sometimes cost less (more on that later), so you might avoid this problem by taking classes year-round. And if you graduate sooner as a result, you'll definitely save money.

If your college requires all freshmen or underclassmen (freshmen and sophomores) to live on-campus, or if you just want to be on-campus for other reasons, one way to save money is to apply for a resident assistant position. Those usually come with free housing and a private room. If you move off-campus in a future school year, I suggest you live nearby. Keeping your commute short and sweet lowers your transportation costs while allowing you to approximate the benefits of on-campus living (access to faculty, study sessions, and so on). But living off-campus is a great way to lower expenses, develop money management skills, and take more ownership for your life. Paying for groceries, utilities, and niceties like Internet or TV gives you a sense of control. You get to see how your actions impact your bottom line and how spending less in one area leaves you more for something else. You see where your money is going, and you learn that you have the power to spend less by using less.

A Housing-Related Financial Aid Snafu

One of the problems with relying on financial aid is that it makes you subject to its weird machinations, like the fact that students who play video games all summer get more aid than those who work hard and earn more than $6,310. Another idiosyncrasy is that some colleges use one figure (say, $9,000) for the cost of room and board if you live *off-campus* and a larger figure (say, $15,000) for the cost of living *on-campus*. Those who move off-campus in this scenario lose $6,000 worth of financial aid eligibility. Just like that. Yes, I know — the whole point of moving off-campus was to save money!

It wouldn't be bad if they took the $6,000 out of whatever loans were in your financial aid package — and let you keep all the grants, scholarships, and work-study. But it's more likely you'll lose some money from each pot.

The good news is that you can anticipate this issue in advance. Just look under "tuition, fees, and estimated student expenses" at the NCES College Navigator (http://nces.ed.gov/collegenavigator). Under "living arrangements," you can compare the figures for on-campus, off-campus, and off-campus with family. Then talk to the financial aid office to make sure an off-campus move will lower your expenses.

Food

Campus dining has come a long way. An increasing number of colleges are putting in ornate, spacious cafeterias, featuring a wide selection of high-quality choices. There's no doubt all this wonderful food, in an architecturally beautiful environment, is an effective recruiting tool. Even when I was a student, we could always tell when prospective students were on campus; the food was much better on those days.

I'm all for raising the bar on campus dining from the garbage I ate, but I wonder if the pendulum has swung too far. If you're borrowing money for college, understand that spending $10 or more per meal adds up quickly. To give you some perspective, take the semester meal plan price and divide it by four to get the approximate monthly price.[4] Compare that figure to what your parents spend monthly to feed your entire family.

In fairness, meal plans are extremely convenient, especially at colleges that allow you to eat breakfast at 10:00 a.m. and lunch at 3:00 p.m. When I was a student, there was a narrow window during which each meal was served. I'd often get stuck somewhere, lose track of time, and miss a meal. That's rarely the case anymore, since many dining halls have gone to a "continuous feed" model from early morning to 8:00 p.m. or so. There's also the "all you can eat" factor, which is fun, but financially a loss for the majority of students who are subsidizing a few large, high-metabolism young men.

If I were living on-campus, I'd get a mini-fridge, and I'd buy some

fruit and cereal (or energy bars in bulk)—that'd be my daily breakfast. I'd pay for no more than ten to fifteen meals per week and look
for cheap restaurants and snacking to cover the rest. (You're probably
going to eat out once per week with your friends anyway.) I'd look to
move off-campus as soon as possible, at which point I'd skip the dining hall altogether. I'd take turns with my roommates when it came
to shopping and cooking, split the bill on common items purchased
in bulk from places like Costco or Sam's Club, cook large portions
(to avoid having to cook as often), and use leftovers for other meals.
Most colleges make microwaves available in the commuter lounge or
in some of their dining areas. You'd probably eat healthier this way
than in the cafeteria, where many freshmen put on the proverbial
fifteen pounds. You'd definitely spend less, provided you weren't
buying endless pizzas.

An in-between solution would be to live in a co-op. Co-ops are
housing arrangements in which students enjoy generous discounts
on room and board in exchange for putting in about five hours per
week in kitchen-related or other household duties.

Recreation

It's easy to spend a ton of money on recreation, but you don't have
to. Think of all the free options you can access, like a pickup game of
Ultimate Frisbee or something more formal, like intramural sports.
If spectating is more of your thing, most universities allow students
free access to sporting events, such as football or basketball games.
There's also an old-fashioned pastime: turning off all your electronic
gadgets and curling up with a good book. Reading is one of those
rare activities that can relax you while stretching your mind—and
it's free if you have access to a good library.

Then there are student clubs of all sorts. For a small fee you can
sample activities ranging from hiking, kayaking, and rock climbing
to visiting museums and attending concerts and plays (while making
friends with students who share your interests). Finally, when you're
out and about, don't forget to check for a student discount. It never
hurts to ask.

Alcohol

Far too many students place an unhealthy premium on alcohol consumption. About 80 percent of students drink, but what's more alarming is that about half of these students binge-drink at least occasionally. That means they're drinking to get drunk and to get drunk fast. As a Christian, I object because God forbids drunkenness (see Proverbs 20:1; Ephesians 5:18), and for good reason. Too much alcohol makes a person lose control, act foolishly, and engage in high-risk behavior. Though offering a short-term thrill, drunkenness leads to long-term pain and regret. Even more sobering, a 1994 study showed that alcohol is involved in 66 percent of college student suicides, 90 percent of campus rapes, and 95 percent of campus violent crime.[5] Moreover, alcoholism later in life has often been traced to habits first formed in college.

Here's another downer: Students waste a ton of money on beer! It's widely reported that college students spend more on alcohol than they do on books, soda, coffee, juice, and milk combined.[6] But here's what they don't tell you: Not everyone is doing it. One-third of college students who drink do so less than once a month.[7] Combined with the 20 percent of students who never drink, that means more than half of all college students drink infrequently at most. Why not join them? If you're of age and wish to occasionally and responsibly enjoy a cold one, go for it. But otherwise focus on your work, save money, and find other ways to have fun with your friends. Bonus: The next day you'll remember what you did.

Textbooks

You probably know that new books are expensive, especially if you buy them in a brick-and-mortar store. But I've noticed another extreme: students refusing to acquire textbooks at all. Some professors require multiple textbooks, even ones they'll barely have you touch all semester. In those cases, it's smart to utilize the library (and your interlibrary loan privileges). I require only one book in each class I teach. And I make sure it's available as a paperback and as an e-book. But I still have students who refuse to get it. Then they get mad at me because their mere attendance, combined with Wikipedia, doesn't lead to full mastery of the course content. Please don't go there. It's not fair to your professor, and you'll only be shooting yourself in the foot. Borrowing, renting (see Chegg.com), or buying used or electronic textbooks are all good options.

You can sell back your books at the end of the semester to recoup some of your money. Check out resale options, and compare buying to resell with renting. In my experience, reselling only gets you a small fraction of what you paid. And you *will* lose money if you end up needing to repurchase the book. So I suggest holding on to well-written, required texts for key courses in your major, if at all possible. Another benefit of keeping books is that you can mark them up as much as you want. Your markings will save you time if you refer to the books in future courses.

A money-saving trick is to buy version 6 of a textbook for which your professor is using version 7. Inside secret: They're often almost identical, but the publisher is looking to make money by pushing thousands of students into an updated edition, for which there are not yet used versions floating around on the Internet for pennies on the dollar. Lastly, sometimes professors put an extra copy of their textbook on reserve in the library, which means you can read it there, but probably not check it out. It never hurts to explore your options before making a purchase.

Jennifer's Story

I paid for most of college myself, usually working two part-time jobs while taking as many classes as was allowed. When it came to spending, I knew I *needed* to stay within my budget! I bought used books online, rented from Chegg, or shared with a classmate when it was an expensive book I knew I wouldn't need for reference later.

After one week into my sophomore year—and nearly $30—of taking the train, I decided to buy a bike. That ended up saving me at least $80 per month. I also dropped the campus meal plan and saved money by cooking for myself, budgeting roughly $200 per month for groceries. My junior year, I moved off-campus to save money, but it backfired because there was a $1,000 per semester penalty fee for nonseniors moving off-campus.

Along the way I also tried to limit my recreation spending. Beyond my many part-time jobs, I had two internships during college. Neither was paid, but one turned into a job that has become my career. Eight months after graduating, I only have $1,200 left in federal loans!

Transportation

If you live on-campus, don't assume you'll need a car. A bicycle, skateboard, or RipStik will probably do the trick. And not having a car means not having to pay for a parking permit or wasting time hunting for a parking space. To get off-campus, take the bus or grab a ride with another student (you can chip in for gas).

Even if you're a commuter, if you live close enough to campus to access everything with something human-powered, don't assume you need a car. If you're saving hundreds of dollars a month by living a bit farther away, public transportation can be a cost-effective alternative to car ownership, especially if you're in a dense, populated city. You can economize on time too by studying on the bus or train.

If you can get all your classes to be on, say, Mondays, Wednesdays, and Fridays, that cuts down on the number of commutes you need to make. It also frees up a couple of days each week to focus on studying, your off-campus job, or taking care of household/family-related duties.

Tuition

Earlier I mentioned that summer classes sometimes cost less, which means you might want to sign a twelve-month, off-campus housing lease, take classes year-round, and graduate sooner. Summer classes are less expensive partly because of supply and demand. Colleges prefer to utilize their facilities all year long—it's good stewardship—but since fewer students tend to take summer courses, lower prices are used to encourage enrollment.

The other reason for discounting summer tuition is that financial aid is more complicated to obtain. Why? To qualify for federal student loans, you must be enrolled at least half-time. If you're planning to take just one class per summer session while working a full-time job, that's not going to cut it. But more significantly, the financial aid office tends to divvy up any federal loan money to which you're entitled over your fall and spring semesters. The same is done with other forms of aid (scholarships, grants, work-study). As we discussed in Trap 5, the Federal Stafford and Perkins loan programs have annual caps. So if you've already tapped your federal student loan money for the year, private loans are your only option for borrowing.[8] Colleges recognize—correctly—that this would deter students from taking summer classes, so they knock down their tuition accordingly. This is especially true of private colleges, which usually have higher sticker-price tuition figures for the fall and spring semesters but rely on discounting to arrive at lower net prices. In the summer sessions, lower prices are published because students aren't accessing discounts.

If you take three classes in each of three summers, you'll be covering about a year's worth of material. So you could potentially graduate as much as a year earlier, resulting in a double bonus—one year *less* of paying for college, and one year *more* of earning money in the workforce.

If your college doesn't offer the classes you need in the summer, perhaps you can take them online from a college that does and transfer back the units. Most colleges allow students to transfer up to some maximum number of units, and online classes usually offer greater flexibility and lower per-unit costs. For academic reasons, it's better to do this with courses outside your major.

Keep in mind that if you're paying tuition by the *unit*, you'll pay more if you take an extra class and less if you don't. But if you're paying by the *semester*, then you can max out on the number of units you're taking. I once took twenty-two semester units. The school didn't charge me a penny extra for going above eighteen units (the usual cap), and doing so helped me graduate a semester early. The workload was painful, though. Just make sure you have enough time to survive, given whatever else you've got on your plate.

Fees

Regarding fees, some universities load up your bill with ones that are, upon request, removable. Zac Bissonnette, a graduate of the University of Massachusetts, was able to remove a few optional fees from his bill by studying each line item and noticing that some were going to various campus organizations that didn't have other ways to collect funds.[9] This seems to be more common at large public universities. Regardless, the point is simple: Study your bill carefully. If you see any fees that look questionable, politely ask your college to explain them. Then ask if they can be removed or waived.

Saving and Giving

Saving and giving are natural components of a budget—crazy as they may seem at this stage of your life. Saving can prevent you from becoming a burden to others when you're hit with an expense you may or may not have anticipated (see Proverbs 6:6–8; 21:20). That's why putting money into savings is worth doing, even if it's only a few hundred dollars per year. For giving, the Old Testament gives us the concept of the tithe, which simply means "a tenth part." Not all Christians see 10 percent as a strict requirement in the New Testament era, but all Christians affirm the concept of proportional giving: As we earn more, we should give more.[10] Some of you reading this sentence are neck-deep in debt and have little to no income;

others don't have it quite so bad. This isn't the place to tackle all the issues related to giving, but it's a topic every Christian must wrestle with. Look over the relevant Scriptures, pray about your situation, choose an amount to give that stretches you without breaking you, and then stick with it.

If you're fairly broke, a good place to start may be to give a dollar for every dollar you save. Whatever you do, don't say, "I'll start giving when I'm *really* making money." It's actually easier to learn to give earlier in life—when our income is low—than it is to learn later. Habits become ingrained and prove difficult to change when we're dealing with bigger numbers. Giving helps us remember that everything we have comes from God (1 Corinthians 4:7). Giving makes possible the work of local churches and important ministries throughout the world. Giving teaches us to trust God to meet our needs. And giving helps us fight greed, anxiety, and materialism. These are all reasons to start giving now.

When classes are in session, you'll probably need all the money you're earning and then some to cover your tuition and living costs. That's understandable. Replenish yourself in the summer by making as much money as possible, working fifty-hour weeks if necessary, as I mentioned in the last chapter. Could you put even $1,000 each year into savings? That's less than $100 per month, but it'd go a long way. What if you put away $500 per year into short-term savings (to cover unforeseen or postgraduation expenses) and the other $500 into retirement savings?

Retirement! Am I kidding? No. Consider this: If at age eighteen you put $500 into a Roth Individual Retirement Account (IRA) and did it again when you were nineteen, twenty, and twenty-one, *after which you never saved another penny (not that I'm recommending that)*, at age sixty-five you'd have … $153,776.[11] Not too shabby. But if you wait until you're twenty-two to perform this four-year saving experiment, the figure drops to $105,024 (almost $50K less). The math of compound interest does not lie: The earlier you start saving, the better.

Having looked at the various spending categories, let's now explore how to manage your spending through the use of a budget.

Manage Your Spending by Using a Budget

Making and using a budget is not as hard as it sounds. It's simple, actually. The first step is to track how you currently spend your money. With a few minutes of daily effort, you can do this for free on Mint.com, with Microsoft Excel, or with some similar program. Next, set measurable targets for each category of your spending: housing, food, clothes, transportation, entertainment, and so on. These targets hold you accountable to drive down specific expenses as much as possible. A lot of students overspend on food, clothes, travel, and entertainment, in part because they don't hold themselves accountable. By the way, why pay a dime for cable TV? There are other things to do, and there's plenty of free or pay-per-use entertainment.

I'm reluctant to provide a sample budget, since any specifics may quickly become outdated. Also, geography is a big factor. Cities like New York, San Francisco, and Los Angeles have much higher living costs than, say, Lincoln, Nebraska. But I still think a concrete example will help.

So here's a set of monthly figures. For tuition, room, and board, let's again take the 2014–2015 figures published by the College Board for an in-state student at a four-year, public institution (tuition and fees: $9,139; room and board: $9,804).[12] I just converted them to monthly amounts and divided the room and board figure into $550 for housing and $250 for food (a best guestimate). I haven't accounted for any savings associated with off-campus living. For textbooks, I'll assume you're employing the kinds of creative strategies outlined earlier.

Housing (including utilities)	$550
Food	$270
Entertainment	$75 (do lots of free stuff and leverage student discounts)
Textbooks/Supplies	$100
Transportation	$75
Tuition & Fees	$765
Clothes/Miscellaneous	$65
Total	**$1,900**

This monthly budget scales to $22,800 for the year. Accounting for saving, giving, and taxes, it'd be nice to bring in more like $30,000 per year. Impossible? After all, we ran the numbers in Trap 6 and only got up to $15,000 per year of earnings! A few thoughts before you throw your hands up in the air:

1. If your EFC is lower than your college's published tuition and fees figure, you have a great chance of qualifying for state or federal grants. The average *net* price of an in-state, four-year public university was estimated as $3,030 in 2014–2015 (compared to a *published* price of $9,139). That means, on average, in-state students at four-year public universities saw annual expenses that were about $6,000 lower than reported in my sample budget.

2. What about help from relatives? I just spoke with Hannah. She's eighteen, has an EFC of $5,800, and is on her way to a private Christian college whose total cost of attendance is about $43,000 per year. The college is only expecting her to contribute $15,000 — much more than her EFC but much less than her actual costs. Her parents and grandparents will pay for half ($7,500); she'll borrow $3,500 through a subsidized Federal Stafford loan and earn the rest via work-study and an off-campus job.

3. If you lived at home while attending a community college and had free room and board during that time, you could save about $10,000 per year by working the kinds of hours we've discussed (more in the summer, less when classes are in session). You'd be building considerable savings *and* reducing your time at a more expensive four-year school.

You *can* control your expenses, but you need to take stock of your situation, make a plan, and then proceed with discipline on both the spending and the earning sides of the equation.

John's Story

I commuted twenty minutes from home to campus to avoid the cost of a dorm and meal plan. I bought a lunch box that was almost an ice chest so I could pack lunch and dinner, if needed. I never knew what books I'd need until right before the semester began. So I'd buy my books from the bookstore on credit, go home to see what better deals I could find online, then return the unopened originals to the bookstore for a full refund. At the end of the semester, I'd almost always sell my books to the highest bidder.

I spent as much time on campus as possible to avoid wasting gas money going back and forth. When I had big gaps between classes, I resisted the urge to go home, where my computer and TV were calling my name, and instead studied, did homework, swam laps in the pool, or just stuck my feet out of the window of my car and took a nap.

All this helped to keep my expenses low. More importantly, it helped me understand where my money was going. Now that I've graduated, these habits have stuck with me and continue to help me make decisions that, together, add up to big savings.

What about a Credit Card? The Truth about Your FICO Score

Millions of students sign up for credit cards each year. Is it the convenience? If so, why not get a debit card instead? They're just as convenient, and they're easier to get if you aren't generating significant income. Is it the cash-back offers? Maybe. I'll take 3 percent back on gas and food any day. But I suspect the biggest draw is the idea that you need a good credit rating (FICO score) as an adult. *College*, you're told, *is the perfect time to get started*. After all, a good credit rating means you're good with money which means you'll get a low interest rate on a home loan someday. Right?

A good credit rating *does* make it easier to finance a house or anything else. Banks prefer to lend money to those with a history of paying it back. But just because you borrow money and pay it back *does not* mean you're good with money. Maybe you should be earning more or saving more, but your FICO score doesn't measure either. Moreover, a good credit rating—a positive history with borrowing money and paying it back—is *not* the only way to qualify for a home loan. But before we go there, let's spell out three general concerns with getting a credit card as a college student:

1. People spend more with plastic than they spend with cash.[13] This applies to everyone, not just college students. The sheer ease with which we can buy stuff with credit cards makes us less conscious about how much we're buying and how much we're spending on what we buy. We're less sensitive to price because we don't *see* the money leaving our pockets. Merchants know this too. That's why most are more than willing to eat the small commission charged by Visa, MasterCard, and American Express.[14] It's not a problem; they've already tacked on that commission to the price of their items. We didn't notice, because their competitors all did the same thing. Credit cards are also known to boost impulse purchases—like the junk food and silly magazines smiling invitingly to you as you wait to pay the cashier in the front of a store.

2. Many college students with credit cards are carrying a balance. It'd be one thing if you never overspent, never made an impulse purchase, and always paid off your entire credit card bill at the end of the month. Then you'd come out ahead with all the cash-back incentives. But if everyone did that, would Visa, MasterCard, and American Express be the highly profitable companies they are? The truth is, most people fall short in one or more of these areas. The more you screw up, the more money the credit card companies stand to make from you.

I'll put this bluntly: Young, cash-strapped college students are a prime target for credit card companies. Why? Because you have little savings (so you're more likely to take on debt), little financial training (so you're more likely to make impulse purchases), and large expenses relative to your income. Many students with credit cards are carrying a balance, which means they're digging a hole fast with double-digit interest rates. The minimum payment line on a credit card bill is beyond ridiculous. If that's all you pay, your debt will quickly snowball. *You must pay the entire balance on a credit card bill every month to avoid foolishly accumulating massive interest.* The interest rate on a credit card is so high that I cannot think of a good reason to ever incur it.

3. You don't know what the future holds. Even if you have income and can qualify for a credit card without a cosigner, is that income stable? What if classes get too demanding and you need to cut back on hours? Or what if, as a part-time worker, your position gets cut during tough times? You don't know what the future holds, so don't spend money that isn't already in your bank account. That's the only thing a credit card allows you to do that a debit card can't do.

But don't you need a good credit history to get a home loan someday? The answer is no, you don't. What you need is a track record of being a responsible person. A lender will be impressed if (1) you have a long history of making timely, full payments on your bills (your rent, phone, utilities, auto insurance, and so on); (2) you have enough savings to make a down payment of at least 20 percent (the more you put down, the less risk for the bank); and (3) you have a stable source of income that's at least three times what your house's mortgage payment would be.[15]

If you never get a credit card or buy anything on debt, you'll be one of the sixty million-plus Americans with no credit score. Having a *low* credit score means you're lousy at borrowing money. That's bad. Having *no* credit score means you don't borrow money. Nothing wrong with that.

Maybe you're like me. You use a credit card, don't overspend, and always pay your balance in full every month. Good for you. My point is that you shouldn't feel the need to own a credit card. They often bring more pain than good, especially for college students. That alone should give you pause. Moreover, you can get a good credit score by having *one* credit card open for just six months. Why not wait until after graduation to get your first card? As it is, you'll need more than six months to save up for a down payment on a home.

If you have a credit card, and a month goes by where you aren't able to pay your bill in full, immediately tear up the card and work like a dog to pay back every penny you owe as quickly as possible. And use a debit card instead. It mercifully forces you to live within your means.

One last caution: Never put college-related expenses on a credit card and then fail to pay the bill in full at the end of the month. That's a classic error too many students make. The interest rates on credit cards are in the 13 to 15 percent range, about *three times* the rates on federal student loans. So you're far better off using federal student loans for college expenses than using a credit card. But if you follow the principles in this and the last chapter, you may not need either.

The Bottom Line

Getting a degree without going broke is like a war fought on multiple fronts. You need to avoid overspending on a college, pursue an educational path that makes sense for you, and earn money while lowering spending during your college years. Far too many students add consumer debt to student debt, putting themselves deeper in the hole and making it harder for them to achieve financial freedom. Do what you need to do, but look for creative ways to do it for less. Don't spend money on yourself that you really don't have. Living with discipline today will set the stage for financial freedom in the years to come. That's what Traps 8 and 9 are about.

Far too many students add consumer debt to student debt, putting themselves deeper in the hole and making it harder for them to achieve financial freedom.

PART 4
KEEPING IT GOING
SUCCEEDING AFTER COLLEGE

TRAP 8

FINDING A HIGH-PAYING JOB WILL BE A BREEZE

Set yourself up for professional and financial success

Dan was excited to be finally graduating. It hadn't been easy, but he'd managed to notch a 3.5 GPA from a reputable state university, not bad for a biology major working part-time every semester. Mom and Dad had covered most of his tuition, so he only had about $13,000 in federal loans, half of which were subsidized. *That's nothing*, he figured, especially since he had six months before his first payments were due. In the last month, Dan had applied for a few job openings in his home state of Minnesota. Now that classes were out, he planned to move back in with his folks and push out several applications per week. *Something will turn up soon*, he figured.

A week went by and then another. It seemed like every place he looked was getting buried with applications. Other times he'd hear of openings, and within a couple days they'd be filled. *How is that even possible?* Dan thought. He had worked last summer for REI, a sporting goods and outdoor gear store. Dan knew they wanted him back, but he was surprised when they offered him a full-time management position with benefits and an annual salary of $35,000. He was appreciative and told them he'd consider it, although he preferred to find something more directly related to his college studies. But after three more weeks of coming up short looking for a job in biotechnology, engineering, or anything having to do with science, Dan called it quits. Reluctantly, he called REI and said he could start the next week.

The Sobering Truth

Are you like Dan, expecting to land a high-paying job related to your major within weeks of your graduation? Before finalizing your celebratory shopping list, consider two sobering observations from a March 2014 survey of more than two thousand students and recent graduates:[1]

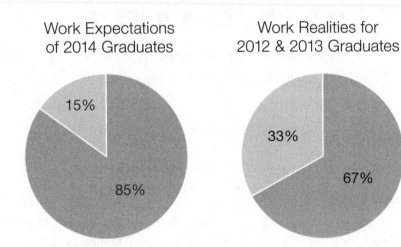

Work Expectations of 2014 Graduates

15%

85%

Work Realities for 2012 & 2013 Graduates

33%

67%

■ Expected to find work in their field
■ Did not expect to find work in their field

■ Were currently employed in their field
■ Were currently not employed in their field

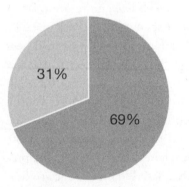

31%

69%

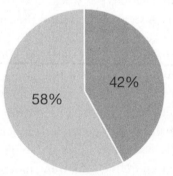

42%

58%

■ Expected to find work within six
  months of graduation
■ Expected it to take longer

■ Found work within six months of graduation
■ Took longer to find work

While 85 percent of the class of 2014 expected to find work in their chosen field, when we look at 2012 and 2013 graduates, only 67 percent of them were currently employed in their preferred discipline. And while 69 percent of the class of 2014 expected to find work within six months of graduation, only 42 percent of 2012 and 2013 graduates in fact did.

What about salary figures? While 81 percent of the class of 2014 expected to earn more than $25,000 per year, only 59 percent of 2012 and 2013 graduates were earning that much, even one to two years later. A full 25 percent earned *less than $19,000 per year.* And only 20 percent earned over $40,000 per year. Take it with a grain of salt—it's just one survey—but there are plenty of other reports that tell a similar story: Recent college graduates are finding themselves in a tough job market.

We have to face reality head-on. Many recent graduates, like Dan, are forced to start with *underemployment*—taking a job that doesn't require a four-year degree.[2] The good news is that some kinds of underemployment are strategic.

In this chapter, we'll explore what it takes to get a good start in the job market after graduation. The first step is to build identity capital.

Build Identity Capital

In her insightful book *The Defining Decade*, Dr. Meg Jay defines *identity capital* as "what we bring to the adult marketplace ... the currency we use to metaphorically purchase jobs."[3] Jay describes Helen, an art major a few years out of college, who struggled to make it as a freelance photographer and ended up as a nanny to pay the bills. Helen, like Dan at REI, was doing work for which she was overqualified and that was unrelated to what she studied in college. Feeling stuck, she went out and landed two interviews, one at a trendy independent coffee shop, the other as a floater (a.k.a., grunt) at a digital animation studio. The coffee shop seemed "cool and not corporate." The animation studio gig seemed beneath her dignity.

But the animation studio opportunity was the clear winner. Why? Because it came with a ton of identity capital. How does being a nanny or a barista help a young artist move forward? It doesn't. Those jobs don't have the potential to lead to something better. The floater job was work that could go on a résumé, work that added to the *story* of an art major and photographer. It was work that said, *I am serious about entering the creative world*.

In the end, Helen was offered and accepted the job as a floater. Six months later, she moved to a desk. Soon afterward, a movie director picked her up as a cinematography assistant and took her to Los Angeles, where she's been making movies ever since.

The moral to Helen's story is that it's not just about the duties that come with a particular job; it's about what a job *represents*, what the job *says about you*, and whether it can be a *gateway* to a better job and an *entry point* to a meaningful career. The perfect job, if it even exists, is probably not something you qualify for fresh out of school. At this stage, you want work that enhances your identity capital, work that says you're serious about developing skills and growing professionally in a particular industry.

Think of how the organization you'd be working for will look on your résumé, how it contributes to what you hope to become. Even if you start off in a mail room, working for IBM, AT&T, Wells Fargo, or some other well-established company gives you undeniable identity capital. Big companies are also more likely to have new positions open up, if not in your department, then elsewhere in the organization. You'll have an inside track if you do your current job well. Finally, larger companies are more likely to provide training and mentoring than smaller outfits. That's especially important early in your career.

While at REI, Dan should keep his eyes open for science-related jobs, *even if they initially pay less than $35,000*. What matters is identity capital. This is especially true in a day in which many of us go through several jobs in our first decade out of school.

Build Career Capital

Why do twentysomethings do so much job-hopping after college? One reason is that our economy has changed. Jobs are less stable than they used to be, especially if you're the last one in and the low man (woman) on the totem pole. But another reason is that many of you are trying to discover what kind of work stirs your passion. You're reluctant to settle for work that's less than fulfilling. If you have to jump around a bit, so be it. Better to do what you love than be stuck in a lowly cubicle paying your dues for some corporate conglomerate.

I get it. Paying dues is so old-school. Who wants to climb their way to the top of the ladder anyway? All that awaits you is an eighty-hour workweek and an ulcer, right? For many of you, it's not about money and power; it's about doing what you love, trying new things, and spending time with your family and friends.

These are healthy priorities, but they can lead to careless decisions. I've seen friends quit good jobs to chase their dreams. Maybe you have too. They feel trapped working for "the man," as if they're following someone else's plan for their life. So they head off to do something creative — maybe sing in a band, pursue photography, write fiction, or start an eclectic Internet business. What no one tells you is that a lot of these people wind up struggling to make ends meet. Then they become disillusioned, wondering if they made a mistake, and the cycle begins anew.

There's a place for personal discovery in your first few years out of college, but there's also a place for commitment. You can't get good at something if you're constantly hopping from job to job. Excellence comes from doing something for a long time, from persevering. Don't think of it as paying your dues for someone else; think of it as good stewardship of an opportunity God has given you. It's an investment in your skill set, in your career. You're putting in the time to become valuable, to develop *career capital*. Over time, career capital leads to higher earnings. But there's a more fundamental benefit: Career capital can earn you the work-life balance that most of you want. Employers are more disposed to dole out perks like flextime or tele-commuting options if you're chugging out excellent work. Another bonus is that doing your job well makes it more fun.[4]

I don't mean to imply that job-hopping in the first decade of your career is always a mistake. It's advantageous when you leave a job with less identity capital to take a position with more identity capital (either because your new employer is better, the industry is better aligned with your aspirations, or your job responsibilities are greater). About two-thirds of lifetime wage growth happens in the first decade of your career, which is also the time when job switching is most common. Leaving a job to take a better job is not a problem. Even later in your career, the most reliable way to get a salary bump is to take a job elsewhere. What you want to avoid is arbitrary job changes. Those tend to set you back.

The best way to land a better job is to leverage the credibility you earned from doing your current job well. You might be surprised at the transferability of the skills you've developed. On the other hand, if every nine months you're chasing what you *think* you love, you may never do anything long enough to get really good at it. That won't be fun, pay well, or help you secure new and interesting opportunities.

The Power of Freelancing

You don't need to turn down a good job to chase your crazy aspirations. The Internet has leveled the playing field for turning hobbies into side jobs. Whether your passion is to teach guitar, sing, act, or do independent photography, if you can find someone who is willing to pay you for a service, voilà. You've got yourself another stream of income. Freelancing is a great way to explore an interest in the marketplace, all while holding a steady job that keeps a roof over your head. The ease with which you can pursue side income is a great reason not to quit your job to pursue something else. Instead, test-drive your passion in the freelance market. If it works, do more of it; if not, at least you won't starve.

Okay, so building identity capital and career capital are important. But how do you get the nod for that first full-time job in your field? A great way to get a leg up is to research your industry in advance.

Research Your Industry

That's what Jessica, a journalism major, did. Jessica started thinking about her professional development a few years before she graduated. Long term, her dream was to travel the world and report on major stories. She began following the news and researching the leading newspapers, magazines, and cable news networks to keep a pulse on possible job leads. She had a Twitter account that followed the industry's leading journalists and syndicated columnists. She interned at the *Washington Post* the summer after her junior year, contributed to several stories, and made a few solid connections. She kept her LinkedIn profile up-to-date and was a member of two professional organizations.

In the fall of her senior year, Jessica attended a national conference as part of her college's student journalism association. To her relief, she wasn't too nervous chatting with others at the various mixers. Because she had learned a bit about the industry, Jessica found it natural to discuss current events and their media coverage. Even though her GPA was only a 3.10, she came across as intelligent, competent, and sophisticated. She particularly hit it off with Susan, who worked for the *Chicago Tribune*. They kept in touch every six weeks or so afterward. In February, Susan asked Jessica for a résumé, since the *Tribune* was expecting to have a few openings later that spring. After a round of interviews, Jessica was offered a full-time job, which she accepted a week after graduating.

What do we see in Jessica's story? First, she did something few college students do: research the industry they hope to enter. The Internet and social media have made it easier than ever to know what's going on, yet surprisingly few students take the time. Familiarity with the world of news media boosted Jessica's confidence when interacting with journalists like Susan. That, in turn, opened doors.

Jessica's story illustrates three other factors that helped her land a promising full-time job: prior experience, networking, and good communication. Let's explore each of these.

Get Experience

In Trap 6, I mentioned that experiential education—internships, co-ops, on-the-job training—is increasingly important to prospective employers. Why? Because passing your classes just means you're able to read, follow instructions, and spit things out on exams. That's good, even necessary, but it doesn't tell employers much about your professionalism, communication skills, or ability to work on a team.

Previous success in an internship or co-op makes you less of a risk in the eyes of prospective employers. It suggests you'll come up to speed and be productive more quickly, which means they won't have to spend as much time and money training you. That's especially true if the industry or environment in which you worked is similar to the position for which you're applying. In short, give companies every reason to believe you'll be an asset and not a liability.

A slow-growth economy means that with a glut of résumés and 1.8 million or so new graduates each year, employers can be choosy. That's what Dan, our biologist-turned-REI-manager, is bumping up against. To make matters worse, many employers think new graduates lack the skills needed to succeed in the workforce. Complaints range from an inability to set priorities and difficulty being managed to poor communication skills and unprofessionalism. The best way to offset these negative stereotypes is to have a proven track record of success.

What if you didn't get an internship during college? You may have to settle for one after graduation. But that internship can soon be leveraged for a full-time job, especially if it's with a well-established organization. In other words, your future prospects are better if your internship gives you a high degree of identity capital.

Build Your Network

The difference between applying for a job and getting selected for an interview is sometimes more about *who* you know than *what* you know. But networking can seem overwhelming and stressful. Some of us aren't sure where, or even how, to start. We feel intimidated at the prospect of talking to strangers about work and career, especially when so much is uncertain and we aren't sure how we stack up in relation to others. Some of us have misunderstandings about what networking involves. We think it means kissing up to the powerful, pretending to be interested in them, angling for their praise, and then exploiting them.

Let's get one thing cleared up—networking does not mean being a jerk. It's not about using people; it's about connecting with people. The key to being interesting *to* others is being interested *in* others.

The true art of networking is friendliness and generosity. It's about overcoming our natural self-absorption, which is what makes us anxious—we can't stop thinking about ourselves, how we're coming across, and so on. If you're an introvert (like me), it's about making that extra effort to show others they're important. It's about asking questions and listening. It's about relating to people on a human level rather than on a laser-focused, utilitarian, "what can you do for me?" level.

> **Networking is not about using people; it's about connecting with people. The key to being interesting *to* others is being interested *in* others.**

Start with the people you already know, your current network. Here are several examples:

- Update your LinkedIn profile with a brief, professional summary of who you are and what you're seeking. Then send a note to your LinkedIn contacts, alerting them that you're in the job market and politely asking them to think of you if they hear of any leads. Make sure your profile lists your skills and experiences.
- Send a brief e-mail to relatives, family friends, people you know from church, and any other adults in your life along the same lines—you're in the job market and would be grateful for any leads they might have.
- Ask your professors for leads and, while you're at it, LinkedIn recommendations.
- Think of alumni from your college you've either met, corresponded with, or are connected to via a friend. Do they work in the industry you hope to enter? Reach out and ask if you

can buy them a cup of coffee in exchange for an informational interview. (More about that in the next section.)

- Go to conferences, alumni events, and anywhere else where you're likely to meet people in your preferred industry. Be natural, friendly, and engaging. Be honest about what you're looking for (a job or internship), but don't be too pushy or aggressive. Listen for any advice. Politely ask for a business card at the end of the conversation. In fact, you might want to make a business card for yourself, even if you're just looking for a job. For just a few bucks you can print more than you'll ever need. Reach out to them via e-mail no later than the following week to tell them you enjoyed the conversation at such-and-such event. Boom, you've just made a new contact.

The idea is to use your current network to expand your network. The people you already know are the best way to get introduced to the people you'd like to know.

Set Up and Conduct Informational Interviews

Informational interviews have become an increasingly popular strategy for job seekers. Unlike a formal interview, in which an organization invites you to meet with them about a specific opening, an informational interview is when *you* make an appointment with an employee to pick that person's brain about his or her career track, company, industry, or whatever the two of you agree to discuss. It's something you can pursue at any time, even if there are no job openings in the company. The goal is simply to establish a better connection with someone in your industry (or in the industry you hope to enter). As Jessica learned from Susan, relationships with people in your industry can end up paying off in unexpected ways.

Ideally, you'd set up an informational interview based on a referral. But before you do, find out if the person has already been given your name and if it's okay to say, "Dr. Hillman referred me." It's often helpful to put the name of a mutual contact in the subject of the e-mail. That way the person is more likely to open the note and read it. It's also good if your mutual contact can help you identify a point of connection that you can use to build rapport in the conversation. For example, are you from the same hometown? Do you share an alma mater? Enjoy the same sport? Cheer for the same team?

Research the person on LinkedIn and elsewhere before making contact. What's his job title? How long has she been at her current employer? Where else has he worked? Where did she go to college? And so on. Research the company too. Once you're ready, reach out to the person and ask if you can schedule an informational interview, either at their office or at a nearby coffee shop.

Bring a list of questions and a pad of paper. Don't just kick back and say, "So, tell me what you do." That communicates, "I was too lazy to prepare for this meeting." And don't just ask black-and-white questions that are easily answered with a Google search. Ask open-ended questions that tap into the overlap between the person's expertise and your professional aspirations. It's helpful to have a brief elevator pitch that succinctly conveys your goal. Something like, "I'm about to finish my degree in architecture from the University of Illinois. I interned last summer at Perkins+Will, working on a contemporary design for an office complex. I'm now looking for a full-time architecture position, preferably in the Chicago area."

Keep in mind that the goal of an informational interview isn't to land a formal interview or even to submit a résumé. The goal is simply to learn. That said, if the person mentions any names of companies that are hiring or people you should contact, jot down the information and follow up accordingly.

Send your interviewee a thank-you e-mail within twenty-four hours of your meeting. That way, it's still fresh in the person's mind. But do not attach a résumé to your note unless one has been requested. It's too presumptuous. It wouldn't hurt to ping this person with another short e-mail in two to three months, just to communicate how you're doing. Sending a note to a key contact three to four times per year keeps you on that person's radar without your becoming a nuisance. And don't forget to thank the person who helped you set up the meeting.[5]

The Benefits of a "Small Ask"

People make two common mistakes in networking. The first is to ask for too much, too soon. If you haven't yet built the relational capital to make a complicated, time-consuming request, doing so can sabotage a new relationship. It's a mistake confident, assertive, and extroverted people sometimes make.

The second mistake is probably more common: to assume that a friendship must be established before you can ask for anything. If you're a twenty-three-year-old recent graduate and the other person is a forty-five-year-old professional, recognize that a friendship may never be formed except by your asking for something.

With people who know us well, the more they like us, the more inclined they are to help us. With more distant relationships, the opposite has been found: If they help you with a small favor, they start to like you.[6] I've been on both ends of these exchanges many times, and I've found it to be consistently true. So go ahead and ask for something. But respect the person's time. Make it a small ask — something simple and specific, something that won't take too much time or energy on the other person's part. Make it easy for him or her to say yes — that's already what most people want to say.[7] Follow up with a thank-you note, and look for a way to return the favor (if you can). That's how relational capital gets built.

Communicate Clearly: Résumés, Cover Letters, and Interviews

Assuming you meet the basic qualifications for a job, standing out to employers is all about a professional presentation on your résumé; a compelling, coherent story in your cover letter; and an intelligent, engaging personality in the interview.

Résumé. You want your résumé to be easy to scan and well organized, and it should communicate that you're somebody who's interesting and can add value. Succinctly list your skills. Include a few sentences for whatever jobs you've held, giving particular emphasis to what *your employer* gained through your contributions. Ideally, there's a connection between your contributions and your professional skills. This connection won't be as tight if you worked as a waiter through college but can now write code and create mobile phone apps. Still, you can convey that as a waiter you learned to be customer-oriented and attentive. Include any significant honors you've received, names of professional organizations you're in, and leadership positions you've occupied. Check the spelling and grammar several times. Then take it to the staff at your college's career center and politely ask if they'll review it. It shouldn't be longer than one page unless you have significant work experience outside college.

> **Standing out to employers is all about a professional presentation on your résumé; a compelling, coherent story in your cover letter; and an intelligent, engaging personality in the interview.**

Cover letter. Tell a compelling story about who you are, what you want, and why *they* would be better off giving it to you. You are not a beggar. You have something to offer! You have an acquired understanding of your interests and talents, and your experiences working and studying in these areas have prepared you for the specific job for which you're applying. You want the prospective employer to read your letter and think, *It makes sense that this person is applying for this job. It's not just a shot in the dark.* The letter should be engaging and have a clear narrative arc. It should be professional but also personal and interesting. That way it's more likely to stand out and hold their attention.

In terms of nuts and bolts, I'd suggest three paragraphs, double-spaced, one or two pages maximum.

The first paragraph is high level. Show a historical trajectory to the interests and talents you're claiming, going back months, if not years, and culminating in your writing to express enthusiastic interest in the open position. If necessary, include a sentence or two explaining any gaps or anomalies in your résumé.

The second paragraph is nitty-gritty. What past accomplishments have you had that suggest you'd be successful in the position? Be specific, objective, and organization-centered. It's not about you; it's about how you added value to your prior organizations and how you'd add value for the prospective employer. For example, Jessica should *not* say, "I really enjoyed my internship last summer at the *Washington Post*. I'm confident it has prepared me for the full-time opening you've advertised." Confident based on what? Here's the kind of thing she should say: "Last summer I researched and contributed to ten original stories for the *Washington Post*, each of which received above-average online traffic, resulting in 20 percent more advertisement revenue." In other words, speak to the interests of your reader. Understand what he or she values.

The third paragraph is brief and concluding. Summarize why you're interested in the job and what you can bring to the organization, thank the person for his or her consideration, and state when you'll be available and how you can be reached (a phone number and an e-mail address).

Interview. Some interviews are more personal, while others are more professional. But they're always some of both. On the personal front, the interviewer wants to know how you present yourself, what you're like. Are you easy to talk to or off-putting? Cold and aloof, or warm and friendly? A professional appearance, arriving on time, smiling, making good eye contact, listening well—all these are crucial. On the professional front, the interviewer wants to know if you can meaningfully discuss your prior academic and professional experiences. And he or she is assessing the value of those experiences.

A common interview style, and one that's easy to prepare for if you know about it, is the *behavioral interview*. My wife was a manager for many years at a Fortune 500 company. She led many behavioral interviews and helped me prepare for mine when I was completing my PhD and hitting the job market. Here's how they work: You'll get a question like, "Tell me about a time you had to work under pressure." Or, "Tell me about a time you had to work with someone who really got on your nerves." Or, "Tell me about a time you accomplished something you're really proud of." The working assumption behind these questions is that past performance is a good indicator of future performance. Makes sense, right? Interviewers are looking for reasons to believe you'd do well in their organization. Your answer should tell a story about a specific *situation*, your *response*, and the *outcome*. They probably won't use these exact terms in their question, but I guarantee they'll be listening for these three elements. Feel free to take some time before answering this kind of question.

With regard to the situation, give the interviewers context. Briefly set the stage for them. Class projects and experiences in prior jobs, even menial ones, provide good examples. I like to identify a time when there was a clear obstacle to overcome. It makes for a good story that can quickly and easily be told. You want to provide a window not just into your *competence* but into your *character*. Interviewers are looking for both.

For the response, it's okay to admit you were anxious about a big presentation or scared that something wouldn't go right on a term project. It's what you do with those emotions that employers want to see. Do your nerves paralyze you, or can you face your fears and get the job done? (Maturity/self-mastery.) Do you go the extra mile, not because you have to, but because you value excellence? (Intrinsic motivation.) Are you constantly behind the eight ball, or do you chip away at large assignments? (Ability to prioritize, plan ahead, and persevere.)

Finally, the outcome. How did the situation/problem turn out? Don't be too subjective here. Remember, it's not about you; it's about serving your organization. What was the result *for the team* or the company? It's not just about the quality of the work — though that's important; it's about how your response was helpful for your boss, professor, coworkers, church, company/organization, or whomever your "customer" was.

Prepare for your interview by rehearsing the kinds of questions you might be asked and what answers you'd give. For example, when I was interviewing, I wrote out five to ten examples I wanted to have at the tip of my tongue. Ask a friend, professor, or mentor to conduct a mock interview, especially if you're getting ready for your first one. Even if the interviewer doesn't ask the exact questions you've practiced with, the rehearsal will have prepared you to think on your feet and to speak in terms of situation, response, and outcome.

Three big interview no-nos: First, *don't take over the interview.* It's *their* show; you're a guest. You'll likely have a few minutes at the end to ask questions—wait for them to indicate that it's your turn, and respect their "time's up" cue. Second, *don't ask questions that might come across as accusatory or critical,* like why the company's stock price nosedived over the last three months. No one will be impressed you did that bit of research. Instead, ask questions that convey you're trying to figure out how your work would contribute to the organization's mission. That's how you want to come across. Which brings me to my third no-no: *Don't present yourself as a self-absorbed, power-hungry money grubber who's looking out for no. 1.* Don't badger interviewers with questions about the salary range, benefits, and how quickly you can get promoted. Let them bring up those topics when they're good and ready. You're there to be an asset, not a leech. Save any negotiating for later.

Negotiate Respectfully

Dan was thrilled to finally land a science-related job offer a year into his job at REI. At a church barbecue that summer he was introduced to Jordan, a research scientist at Medtronic. They hit it off, and Dan made an effort to keep in touch. One day, Jordan e-mailed out of the blue with a link for an open "Lab Technician, Level I" position. Dan applied, interviewed, and got the green light. Assuming he accepted the offer, Dan would start immediately and receive a salary of $33,000 per year, plus benefits. Based on his performance, he could get promoted to a research scientist position in three years, even without a master's degree.

Dan texted his dad the details. "Only $33,000?" his dad shot back. "That's less than what REI started you at! You should definitely ask for more." The thought terrified Dan. After a year at REI, he didn't want to do anything to jeopardize the offer. Sure, the pay wasn't great, but Dan loved the identity capital that would come with the job. And Jordan told him that the promotion to research scientist would come with a good-sized pay raise.

In this economy, a lot of us are like Dan. Negotiation makes us queasy. We just want to say yes and get on with it. It's true that in some lines of work, like being a teacher at a public school, salary is determined by a set schedule (a pay ladder) based on your highest degree and years of experience. There's little to no room for discussion. But in most industries there's a fair amount of subjectivity when it comes to determining a person's starting salary.

It's usually a mistake to immediately accept whatever salary you're offered. Most employers will initially offer a figure less than what they'd ultimately be willing to pay. In doing so, they're not being immoral or insulting. They're trying to manage their limited resources. Frankly, they don't know what you're worth. What you'll accept is what you're worth. If they spend a little less money acquiring an employee, that gives them a little more to use for something else. You would do the same in their position.

I know what some of you are thinking: *If Dan asks for more money, can't Medtronic just walk away?* The risk is super-small. Before a company makes you an offer, they've talked about it at great length. Several key people have all given you a green light. They want you. It would be rare—and unprofessional—for an employer to retract an offer because a candidate sought to respectfully negotiate. Now if you're told that the salary is *not* negotiable, that for whatever reason there's no flexibility, and you get angry and demand another ten grand, that's a sure way to burn a bridge.

The key in negotiation is putting yourself in the other person's shoes and understanding his or her perspective and goals, while respectfully standing up for your interests. But again, you're not a beggar here. You have something to offer. Speak to their interests, to what you can do for the company.

Never get offended by a lowball offer. Remember that it's business, not personal. The first thing I'd do is politely respond, "May I please ask how you arrived at that figure?" It may have been a shot in the dark! Don't let that be a showstopper. Knowing how they came up with their salary figure may suggest a line of reasoning that would convince them to raise the number. Consider a few examples:

- Do you have experience or qualifications they may have overlooked?
- Do you have another job offer for more money?
- Are they aware that the average starting salary in that industry, in that part of the country, is in the range of (say) $50,000 to $60,000 (based on some reputable source you can point them to)?
- Is the cost of living in the city where the job is located higher than where you currently reside?
- Do you have a friend graduating at the same time who got offered more money for a similar position?
- Will the job require that you seriously update your wardrobe? (That could be used to negotiate a signing bonus.)

> **The key in negotiation is putting yourself in the other person's shoes and understanding his or her perspective and goals, while respectfully standing up for your interests.**

The way you negotiate is as important as what you negotiate. Confidence doesn't mean arrogance or brashness. You can be polite, respectful, *and* assertive. If you're caught off guard by something they say, fight the temptation to immediately react. Instead listen, ask questions, and learn. Don't get upset or blurt things out that you may later regret. Excuse yourself by saying you need some time to think it over. Do your analysis and decide on a response. Then craft a professional e-mail, politely making your requests and giving the best rationale you can muster. If you're ready to accept the offer if the employer agrees to your requests, there's power in saying that. You're giving him or her a way to immediately accomplish the goal of filling the position and getting back to the million other things on their plate.

Just as you're giving a rationale for your requests, listen to any rationale your potential employer may provide. For example, "You'll be coming in at Band II, and the top of that band is $60,000. My director won't let me go any higher." That's a firm answer that should be respected. If it means you'll have to decline the offer, politely inform the person, giving him or her one more chance to see if an exception is possible. Be aware that it's not uncommon for some things to be negotiable (such as salary and start date) and other details to be nonnegotiable (such as benefits, which are usually set by a corporate policy).

Finally, be careful to preserve the relationship throughout the process. Don't threaten or manipulate. Treat the person you're negotiating with the way you'd want to be treated (Matthew 7:12). It's a small world — you may be turning down a job from that person today but be applying for another in a few years. It's foolish to burn any bridges. Negotiation isn't a blood sport. It's about looking for a win-win.

The Bottom Line

Even though our economy feels like it's limping along, there *are* concrete things you can do to earn money, launch your career, and move toward financial freedom. Researching your industry, getting experience, networking, and good communication can help you land jobs that offer identity capital. You're not a beggar in this process. You have something to offer. But you're not the only candidate, so moderate your confidence with humility. Pray, trust God, and cast your net wide among positions that make sense for this stage in your professional life.

If you have to accept underemployment, fight discouragement. You're not the only one! Pick a job that's most likely to lead to something better. Work hard, be faithful, and keep your eyes open for jobs with more identity capital. At any point, feel free, if you'd like, to try your hand at turning a hobby into a side business. Developing strong, marketable skills (career capital) takes perseverance, but over time, it leads to greater job satisfaction, higher pay, and more autonomy at work.

TRAP 9

I'VE GOT A PAYCHECK AND CAN FINALLY LIVE IT UP!

Live within your means while pursuing financial independence

What if you borrowed money for your undergrad degree—more than you care to admit? Should you move back home to save money? That can be a good option, but it also presents some dangers. Or maybe you're tempted in the other direction. Now that you're making the big bucks, you feel the urge to splurge, spending even bigger bucks. Whatever your debt and income situation, you'll have important financial decisions to make in your first decade after college. And there are some common mistakes you'll want to avoid.

Living On Your Own: How Much to Spend?

Housing (rent) will probably be your number one expense, so it's important to get a sense for what's reasonable. Remember Emily, whose story I told in the introduction? Let's see where her $2,150 monthly budget goes awry:

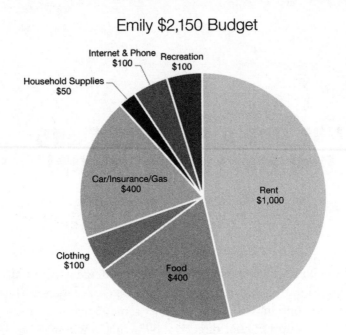

Emily $2,150 Budget

You see the problem? Emily is spending almost half of her take-home pay on rent and utilities. So she has nothing left at the end of the month to pay down her student loans or to build up any savings. If she could cut her rent by a few hundred dollars per month — maybe by getting two housemates instead of one — that'd be a huge improvement.

Because here's the thing: Paying back student loans is not optional; it's something Emily must do. And if she wants to avoid credit card debt when faced with an emergency, she needs to build up some short-term savings too.

What if, in your situation, the only way to accomplish these objectives is to knock down your rent ... to nearly zero?

Moving Back Home: How to Make It Work

The freedom and privacy of living alone are great, but even a one-bedroom apartment can get pricey for someone fresh out of college. If your options for roommates aren't the best, who would blame you for deciding to live with your parents or a relative rather than with a stranger? You probably know someone who moved back in with their folks to save money. Maybe you've done it, or you're thinking about it. If you get along well with your parents and don't feel like you'd be imposing on them, moving back home can make a lot of sense.

But the older you are and the longer you stay, the more likely it is to cause a strain in the relationship.[1] That's because the natural order is being perturbed. You've grown up, maybe left for a few years, are treated like an adult elsewhere in society, and yet live daily with echoes of your childhood. Your parents *want* to treat you like a full-fledged adult, but it can be easier said than done. Your interaction patterns have to overcome habits ingrained over eighteen to twenty-two years. Over time, you may get a gnawing sense that living with your parents is holding you back, depriving you of the opportunity to achieve independence. Or not. Maybe you get comfortable—too comfortable—because your folks are doing things for you that you'd otherwise have to do for yourself. The longer you stay, the harder it may get to consider leaving. Either way, tension or not, the answer is the same: It really is time to go. If not now, soon.

There are exceptions. Maybe one of your parents is out of the picture and the other's health is failing. Mom, Dad, or another ailing relative needs your help, and you get to step up and shoulder responsibility while saving money. Everybody wins there. But in most cases, your journey to responsible adulthood will be stunted by an extended homestay.

So what should you do if finances make it impossible to live anywhere else? Here are three ideas for your consideration:

1. Establish a plan and a timeline. If your goal is to get out, there's nothing like a plan to make it happen. Consider your earning power: Are there freelance or side jobs you can take on to bring in more money? Consider your spending: What can you give up to minimize it? If you have a huge debt load, be laser-focused on knocking off your loans.

Credit card debt is usually worse than student loan debt because of the double-digit interest rates. Ignore the ruse of the minimum monthly payment. Pay your balance in full every month. If you're carrying a balance, throw every extra dollar you have at it. If you're consistently spending more than you have, cut up the credit cards. There's no reason to put more on the plastic that got you in trouble in the first place. Prove your financial restraint for a few years before trying again.

If you took out student loans, you should *at least* be making the monthly payments to avoid any late fees. If you have extra money and don't have higher-interest debt, throw it at your student loan with the *highest interest rate*. Once that loan is dead and gone, direct all the money you were spending on it to the next highest interest rate loan. Note that the faster you pay back your loans, the less it ends up costing you because you minimize the accumulated interest (the amount you're obligated to pay above and beyond what was borrowed).

Make sure you're looking at all your student loans. If you have several from multiple semesters, it's easy to miss one and end up in default, especially if you have both federal and private loans. To make sure you're capturing everything, run a free credit report on yourself. At www.annualcreditreport.com, you can request reports from the three credit bureaus: Equifax, TransUnion, and Experian. You're entitled to one free report per twelve-month period per bureau.[2] Set up a spreadsheet on your computer or dedicate a page in your journal to track your progress and create debt-reduction goals for the next few months.

Lowering spending and retiring debt are two-thirds of the battle. The final aspect is growing your income. If you're chugging out good work for your employer, it may take a few years, but your earnings should rise. Before long, you'll be able to share the cost of an apartment while continuing to pay off the rest of your loans. Or maybe you'll stay at home until you finish the process once and for all.

What about Consolidating Student Loans to Lower Your Payment?

Many people consolidate their federal student loans to create one lower monthly payment. Your consolidated loan interest rate is the weighted average of your current loans.[3] However, consolidation has two significant downsides: (1) Consolidation prevents you from allocating any extra money toward your highest interest rate loan. Any extra payment goes to the aggregated (consolidated) total. But if you had an extra $300, wouldn't you rather have it go toward a loan that is costing you more (the one with the highest interest rate)? (2) While consolidation lowers your monthly payment, it does so by extending the repayment period, which ultimately costs you more (as we saw in Trap 5).[4]

If you absolutely *must* have lower payments, I can see a case for consolidating, although you'll want to compare it to Income-Based Repayment (IBR) or Pay as You Earn Repayment (PAYER), if you qualify for either. The advantage of IBR or PAYER is that your payment is determined by your income, and any debt remaining after the repayment period is forgiven.

If you're thinking of consolidating credit card debt, the same drawbacks apply, plus one more: Consolidation doesn't get you out of debt. You need to change the spending habits that got you in trouble in the first place.

2. Contribute to the household expenses. If the point of living with Mom and Dad is to lower expenses, why chip in a dime unless it's required? Here's why: Apart from the obvious—that it shows appreciation and tangibly helps your parents—if you want to be treated like an adult, you can only be a free rider for so long. Besides, there's plenty of room between zero and the amount you'd have to pay for food, rent, and utilities if you were living on your own. Your family will be spending more on food with you there; you should pay the difference. The utilities and water bill will go up because of you; you should pay the difference. Don't worry about exact figures. Round up, and you're still saving a ton of money.

If your debt load is monstrous — say, more than twice your annual income — and your parents are saying, "Please, we just want to help ... we refuse your money," at least offer yourself as a slave laborer around the house and yard. Take on any chores possible (meal preparation, dishwashing, shopping, laundry, lawn mowing, child care, whatever). The key is that you're contributing, which affects how your parents think of you and, perhaps more importantly, how you think of yourself. That, in turn, will impact how you handle your finances. A passive mind-set does not serve the cause. You will either conquer your debt or be conquered by it.

3. Treat your host like a landlord and respect the household rules. You can be treated like an adult *and* honor household rules. The key is to remember that your parents are doubling as landlords.

When you rent an apartment, you're free to do as you please, as long as you don't break the law or damage the property. But when you rent space in someone else's home, you have more restrictions because your behavior impinges on others. Your folks aren't treating you like a kid if they expect you to turn off the lights, lock the door behind you, or be quiet when you come home late. They would expect that of any tenant who is renting a room in their home.

Sometimes the best way to maintain the relationship is to put expectations in writing and assign reasonable financial penalties for infractions. A little formal perhaps, but it's better than having your parents nag you. Let's say you agreed to mow the lawn every week by noon on Saturday. You forget one week. The next week, your parents start riding you. An e-mail on Thursday. A couple of text messages and a passing comment on Friday. Another text first thing Saturday morning — when you were *just minutes* away from doing it! That would drive me nuts. I'd rather my parents treat me like a landlord would treat a tenant: "If the lawn is not mowed by noon on

Saturday, there will be a $10 penalty (or whatever) for every hour until it's mowed." Nothing personal. Just business. Screw up, and you get a fine. You learn your lesson and change your ways. Nobody gets nagged. Everybody wins.[5]

I also like this model because it's how the real world works. Of course, most homeowners aren't fined for not mowing their lawns (although that might help me take better care of mine). But financial consequences for breaking rules are common. I have an appointment with a doctor this Monday who has the audacity to charge $10 for *every five minutes* a patient is late. Having such a rule is her prerogative. I don't like it, but it's what I'm signing up for when I ask to see her.

It's not always necessary, but professionalizing a relationship helps people treat each other with respect. It gives each party a manner by which to right wrongs without getting bent out of shape. That's often a big plus when you're living with parents/relatives as an adult.

What if living at home isn't an option? In addition to paying down your debt, you'll have to take charge of your spending, getting creative if necessary. To explore how you might do that, let's return to the story of Emily.

Taking Charge of Your Spending

Living at home wasn't going to work for Emily, given the location of her new job. But she leveraged her connections and eventually found two other girls with whom to share a townhouse for $1,800 per month. Even with utilities, her portion of the rent would be about $650. What else might she do to free up cash?

Cook more, dine out less, and eat what you buy. Before Emily moved out, her mom warned her not to spend too much on food. Smart mom. That's one of the biggest mistakes young graduates make, especially if they're single. I get it. You don't know how to cook; you don't want to spend all that time cooking for just one person; and restaurants are convenient and offer a chance to meet up with friends. But there is a price to be paid. Try this: Write down how much per month you *think* you should be spending on food. Then track what you *actually* spend each month. You might be surprised at how different these numbers are.

After a few weeks of getting acclimated to the city, Emily and her housemates went in together on a Costco membership. They started cooking food for several meals together. They packed their lunches. They had leftover nights. Emily cut down her Starbucks addiction to once per week. After discovering that buying groceries after work on an empty stomach led to overbuying, she shifted to after-dinner shopping. When she realized she was throwing away spoiled yogurt and lunch meat, Emily began tracking how much money she was wasting. This reminded her to buy perishables in smaller quantities and to eat all the fruits and vegetables she'd purchased.

Avoid overspending on clothes. Emily used a graduation gift to expand her wardrobe after a chat from a coworker about the unofficial dress policy, which was surprisingly different from what Emily had worn to class in college. Going forward, she hoped her $100 monthly clothes budget would suffice. One month, she spent $95.84 on a couple of skirts and a new pair of shoes—and it was only the fifteenth! The next week, she saw a gorgeous blouse at Nordstrom's that looked perfect for the company picnic that weekend. Should she go for it? Knowing she still had to pay her student loans that month, she held back. Another outfit from her closet ended up working just fine.

Emily learned that delaying a purchase is a good way to figure out if it was necessary. She also learned to purchase items that could be worn on multiple occasions and with lots of outfits. She prioritized and made tradeoffs. For example, she allowed herself one indulgence—a Coach purse—but she *underspent* her clothes budget for several months prior in order to afford it. The other lesson Emily applied, following her housemate Alexis's lead, was to shop for clothes out of season, when they were on sale.

Live on Money You've Already Made

One of the easiest ways to get into debt — even if you made it through college relatively debt-free — is to overspend on your lifestyle as a young professional. Furniture, a flat-screen TV, a new bed, a laptop, a gaming console, travel — you name it. It's easy to think you can live large now that you've landed a real, full-time job with benefits. So you're racking up the points on your credit card, and before you know it — uh-oh, you aren't able to keep up with your payments. You tell yourself, *That's okay; I'll soon be making more money. I'm a few months away from a promotion.* Six months later, the promotion hasn't come, but you've racked up another six grand in fresh debt.

It's not always easy, but it is simple: Don't put your hope in money you *might* make. Live on the money you've already made. Be content. Sure, your parents have a larger house and more stuff than you do, but they make more money. And they've had many more years to save. Be disciplined and work hard, and in ten years you'll be able to do more too.

Shop around. Emily's household supplies budget was $50 per month. At first, she was buying all cleaning supplies, toiletries, and food from the grocery store. But then her housemate Alexis told her how much less she was spending at Target and Walmart for the same items, especially when she could avoid a name brand and buy the store brand. Emily and her housemates also started to clip coupons for things they planned to buy anyway (not just chasing deals for things they didn't need).

Take the maximum number of allowances on your W-4 form. Unhappy about having to do her taxes for the first time, Emily picked up

TurboTax and started playing around with it. She soon discovered she was due a federal tax refund of more than $2,000. *Score!* she thought, texting her dad to share her excitement. That's when he told her she was giving the government an interest-free loan while living all year long on smaller paychecks. Her dad advised her to increase the number of allowances on her W-4. That led to a bump in her take-home pay—extra money she could immediately put to use and still not be behind on her state and federal tax obligations.

Build an emergency fund. In January, a friend of Emily's got engaged and asked Emily to be the maid of honor. How could she say no? But Emily soon found that looking pretty was going to cost her a pretty penny. Then there was a wedding shower and bachelorette party to host! With nails, hair, makeup, and a dress she'd probably never wear again, she was looking at a price tag north of $500. And though she was keeping up with her student loan payments, she hadn't exactly kept a whole lot under her mattress. Her checking account was not paying interest, but even if it were, her balance couldn't handle a major jolt. She could put the wedding expenses on her Visa card, but that seemed scary.

Emily needed an emergency fund. Putting a large, unexpected expense on a credit card is a bad idea because money isn't going to fall from the sky thirty days later when the bill comes due. But the wedding wouldn't be for a few months, and that gave Emily an idea. She had budgeted $400 for gas, auto insurance, and maintenance on her car (a family hand-me-down she had used in college), and that was about the amount she'd been spending. But Emily had discovered that if she left for work twenty minutes earlier, she could take the train and walk to her office. If she did that regularly, it'd run her about $150 per month. If she used public transportation or ride-sharing options, she could probably get around on the weekends for $50 to $100 per month.

After praying about it and talking to her mom, she and her mom came up with a plan. Her parents would sell her car for her, allowing her to pay for her friend's wedding-related expenses *and* create an emergency fund. While technically Emily could have used the extra money to pay down her student loans faster, that choice would have left her without an emergency fund. But as she had discovered, unexpected expenses arise ... unexpectedly. Emily opened an interest-bearing money market with the proceeds of her car sale, and she had a great time at the wedding.

Never lease a car. Emily's friend Mike was impressed by the quick windfall she got from unloading her car. But he had leased a new Ford Mustang, and the lease didn't expire for another year and a half. He had even gone on LeaseTrader.com to see if he could find someone to pick up his lease, but to no avail. Mike had leased the Mustang because he'd always wanted to buy one but couldn't afford it. Now he regretted his decision. Leasing a car is really dumb. It means spending hundreds of dollars every month for a vehicle you do not, and never will, own. And because you're dropping serious cash each month for the privilege of *borrowing* a car, you're less likely to ever build up the savings you'd need to someday *buy* a car. That means you're the kind of sucker who will have to keep leasing cars. Cha-ching every month for the car dealership, but no equity for you.

Perhaps you're wondering, *Equity? Wait, don't cars lose value over time?* Yes, but even an old car can be quite valuable. My fourteen-year-old Honda Accord with 180,000+ miles on it gets me around just fine, and the auto insurance on it is dirt cheap. If you keep leasing relatively new cars, you will pay hundreds of extra dollars on auto insurance *on top of* the lease payment. That's no way to get ahead.

Mike's friend Andy made a similar mistake. He bought a new $30,000 Mazda Miata with $6,000 in savings and a $24,000 loan. A year and a half later, the Miata was totaled in an accident. Nobody was hurt, and it was the other guy's fault, but there was still a problem: Andy's insurance company determined that the value of the car at the time of the accident was $20,000, which was less than the $22,000 Andy still owed on the car. So Andy not only lost his car; he had to cough up an extra $2,000 to close out the loan.

Taking out a loan to buy a new car is foolish. New cars lose a big chunk of their value the moment you drive them off the lot. Your best bet is to buy a reliable used car 100 percent with cash. *Consumer Reports* can help you determine the value of used cars and find out which ones last longer. The average driver puts 15,000 miles per year on a car, so if a well-built vehicle lasts fifteen years, then buying a car with about 45,000 miles on it will still give you twelve years of use.[6] Your used car would cost a *lot* less up front than a brand-new car, and your ongoing insurance bill would be much lower.

Match your employer's 401(k) contribution. Many employers help their employees plan for retirement. A common method is the 401(k) match, where you put in a certain percentage of your salary and your employer puts in a matching percentage, up to a certain amount. It's not always a one-for-one match, but it's almost always something.

A lot of new employees are initially short on cash flow. They need money for food, clothes, rent, and student loan payments—today! Retirement is eons away, so they figure, *I'll put money away for retirement later, when cash flow is not so tight.* But the reason that taking advantage of the 401(k) match is critical, even when you're in debt, is because the benefit of the match is greater than the harm of the interest on your debts. The match is 100 percent gain—free money sitting on the table. And as we saw in Trap 7, compound interest means a little extra today goes a long way over the next few decades.

> **Taking advantage of the 401(k) match is critical, even when you're in debt, because the benefit of the match is greater than the harm of the interest on your debts.**

Sheepishly, Emily called Judy, the nice woman in human resources. "What exactly is the 401(k) match?" Emily asked. Judy replied, "The company contributes one dollar for every dollar you contribute from your salary, up to 4 percent. So if you set aside 4 percent of your salary, you'll max out the benefit," Judy replied. Now that Emily's expenses were under control, she signed up for the full match.

A year into her first job, Emily's monthly take-home pay had risen to $2,250.[7] Here's her new actual budget—what she was *really* spending, not just what she hoped to be spending.

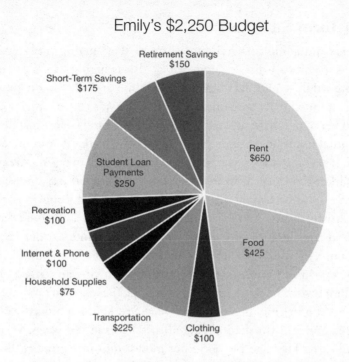

Emily's $2,250 Budget

Retirement Savings $150
Short-Term Savings $175
Student Loan Payments $250
Recreation $100
Internet & Phone $100
Household Supplies $75
Transportation $225
Clothing $100
Food $425
Rent $650

Notice how Emily is now able to set aside $250 per month toward student loan payments (on track to pay these all back in ten years), save $175 per month, contribute $150 per month into her 401(k), and spend a bit more on food and recreation. A much better situation! Within a couple of years, Emily had saved $5,000, at which point she reallocated most of her short-term savings toward paying off her student loans faster. What would that accomplish? It would mean killing off her loans not in ten years but in *seven and a half years*—saving a couple thousand dollars of interest.

Emily's housemate Alexis was in a similar income situation, but without the student debt. That gave her the freedom to work on long-term savings.

Long-Term Savings

Alexis did some research and learned that buying individual stocks is usually a losing strategy.[8] The risk is high — stock prices fluctuate wildly — and she didn't have the time to study the financial outlook of individual companies. She talked to her Uncle Greg, who advised her to purchase no-load, low-fee mutual funds. He explained that mutual funds held hundreds of stocks, which greatly minimized the risk if any one stock performed poorly, while still exposing Alexis to a market-rate return on investment. Greg helped her open an account at an investment firm and even threw in a deposit as an early Christmas gift. An adviser helped Alexis build a portfolio that put her in a position to earn about 7 to 10 percent interest per year. It was a mix of mostly stock-based mutual funds and some bonds.

Do you think Emily did the right thing, applying an extra $150 per month toward her student loans? After all, these weren't required payments she was making. She could have just kept her monthly bill the same and still finished paying off her loans in ten years. What was the rush? Had she put $150 per month into investments, like Alexis did, wouldn't she have made a similar profit?

Here's why I agree with Emily's strategy. While Alexis stands to gain a profit, she's doing so at the expense of risk. Within a five-year span, the stock market usually has at least one bad year. But because Alexis is young and doesn't have any debt, she can afford to adopt a long-term perspective with that money. If there's a loss in the short term, she can just ride it out. But since Emily owes about $20,000, she doesn't have that flexibility. It's not just that applying an extra $150 per month toward her loans saves Emily a couple thousand dollars in interest; it's that it buys her the *certainty* that her debt is retired more quickly. Emily's strategy gets the monkey off her back sooner and frees up future income for living, giving, and saving — including long-term savings. Emily was smart, though, to start on her retirement savings much earlier to benefit from the free money of her employer match.

Speaking of long-term issues, let's close out the chapter looking at three financial decisions that await many of you in the next five to ten years: marriage, buying a house, and whether to attend graduate school.

Debt, Love, and Marriage

What if as you're digging yourself out of debt, you're in a romantic relationship that looks promising? Marriage *should* be on your mind—I mean, that was the point, wasn't it? God didn't wire you with desires for emotional and physical intimacy so you could date someone for ten years. But if you're living with your folks, marriage might be the last thing on your mind. After all, getting married and moving into a place of your own would mean facing your bills. Even if you're out on your own, tying the knot when you have a large debt load hanging over your head may seem frightening and unkind. Maybe you're wondering, *Isn't it better to wait until I can afford to get married? I don't want to saddle my spouse with my money problems.*

Finances are one of those things all couples need to discuss sooner or later. It's important to be honest about your situation. Deception is a bad foundation for any relationship. Getting hitched signs you up for a lifelong three-legged race. You won't get far unless your partner is going in the same direction. And while you absolutely *should* be paying off your debt as much as you can now, nothing says you need to have all your ducks in a row before saying "I do." It's not so much about *where you've been* as *where you're going*. The two of you should be on the same page about getting out of debt, living within your means, saving, and giving—that's what counts.

In fact, if the two of you are making good financial choices, delaying marriage can make things harder. Marriage transforms people. It stretches them, forcing them to grow up in many ways. Marriage can shape you into a more responsible, hardworking, conscientious person—the kind who more quickly gets out of debt. Don't get me wrong. Marriage won't automatically do that for everyone. Plenty of married couples get themselves into a mess with unrestrained spending. But if the two of you are in agreement about how to cut costs and get on your feet, you're at least as likely to do that together as you are to do it apart.

Logistically, married couples pool their resources and can therefore lower their expenses better than if they remained single. You don't merge costs with housemates as much as you would with a spouse. And with family looming on the horizon, two people *who were already going in the right direction* have an extra incentive to get their finances in shape. To be clear, I'm not suggesting going out and getting married to boost your bottom line. If your debt situation is getting worse and you're in denial or if the two of you strongly disagree on how to handle your finances, marriage will only magnify your problems. I'm just saying that if you're taking the right steps now, you don't need to fear marriage for financial reasons.

Buying a House: Good Debt (Usually!)

Someday you'll probably want to own the ground beneath your feet. Yes, there's the hassle of maintenance — though if you're handy or decorative, it's actually fun. And yes, home ownership ties you down. But that's just the point. If you're like most people, you'll get sick of the instability of constantly moving or haggling over the rent. You'll want to lay down roots. The good news is that a house, unlike a car, tends to appreciate in value, so it's not necessarily bad to borrow money to purchase a home.

The money for a down payment on a home should come from your long-term savings, not your short-term reserves. You can buy a house with as little as a 5 to 10 percent down payment, but it's preferable to avoid being required to purchase private mortgage insurance (PMI), an extra expense. That typically means a 20 percent down payment. If you can save $500 per month, you'd have $60,000 in ten years, which is 20 percent of a $300,000 home. If half came from your spouse, you'll get there in half the time. The other benefit of a large down payment is that your mortgage, and the associated monthly payment, will be lower.

People sometimes compare the mortgage on a home to the rent on an apartment, but the comparison isn't quite accurate. With a home, you've also got property taxes and home insurance (which is higher than renters insurance, since it covers not just your stuff but the actual structure of the home as well). You're also responsible for maintenance. Combined, these will probably run several hundred dollars per month. But in the long run, the appreciation of your home will usually more than make up for the associated costs. (Just avoid "creative" remodeling projects that could make your home harder to sell.)

Graduate School: Investment or Distraction?

Advanced degrees have become more common as industries up their requirements and as young professionals look for ways to stand out and earn their way into more lucrative lines of work. How should you assess if graduate school makes sense for you? And how on earth can you pay for it?

Graduate school makes sense if you want a job that requires an advanced degree, or if you're so in love with a subject that you can't see yourself doing anything but study it at a deeper level. Ideally, it's some of both. Since graduate school is a lot of work, it helps if you love what you're learning. Because graduate school is also expensive, it helps if there are jobs on the other side that utilize your extra training.

Graduate school usually raises your earnings power and career prospects, but it narrows your job market in terms of the number of available positions that match your level of training. You also need to consider who your peers will be and how well you'd fit in. Only about three in ten students who earn an academic associate's degree or bachelor's degree go on to earn an advanced degree.[9] We're talking about people who did well in their undergraduate program, people who are academically gifted and inclined, people who want to develop expertise in a particular field and to become knowledge workers at a high level (professors, lawyers, researchers, doctors, and so on). Does that sound like you? Don't just trust your gut; get advice from those farther down the road.

Your professors are the best people to talk to about graduate school because each of them went, and they can compare you to other students. The drawback is that professors tend to clone themselves. They love seeing students follow in their footsteps, so they sometimes overrecommend graduate school. One way to help fight this tendency is to ask your professors how they'd rank you relative to other students they've taught.

Here's why: Your references for graduate school will probably be asked to rank you in exactly this manner (top 10 percent, top quarter, top half, and so on). Unless you did your undergraduate at a selective university, your reference won't really be helpful unless he or she says you're in the top quarter. But trust me — you'd rather find out now than later. Full-time graduate students don't earn much money, and they're giving up what they could be earning in the workforce. In some cases they're *borrowing* money. You don't want to do all that, only to squeak by and then struggle to find work for which you're not overqualified.

So how do students pay for graduate school? Some attend graduate school on weekends and evenings while working full-time. In this scenario, you may be able to get your employer to foot the bill. (I did that for a few classes which I later transferred to the University of California at Berkeley.) Other part-time students pay from their savings or borrow the money. In Trap 5, we discussed the annual and cumulative limits on federal loans for undergraduate students. Additional funds are available for graduate students. Advanced degrees in medicine, law, or business are often financed with massive amounts of debt, but graduates often earn enough to pay off their loans without much hardship.

As with an undergraduate degree, there are online tools to assess your earning prospects. And once again, debt financing should be a last resort. I sometimes hear about students completing their undergraduate program, not finding work, and jumping back in to graduate school to defer their loans. That's a terrible reason to attend graduate school. Sure, your loans are in deferment, but the interest is still accumulating (except on subsidized loans). It's not like you can stay in school forever. You need a plan for how you're going to use all that schooling. Sometimes students overdo it, unaware that once they land a job with identity capital (see Trap 8), they can often climb the ranks just fine without an advanced degree.

Back to paying for graduate school. Thankfully, graduate students have three additional sources of funding to tap: fellowships, research assistantships, and ships. Fellowships are awarded by third-party agencies and generally pay tuition plus a small stipend for living costs. A research assistantship is funded by a professor from one of his or her grants. The job is to conduct original research under a professor's leadership. A ship is funded by a professor's academic department. The job is to help administer a professor's class, perhaps by leading smaller discussion sections for a large lecture course, overseeing the laboratory component of a science or engineering course, or grading papers. Ships generally work about twenty hours per week in exchange for roughly the same compensation that a research assistant or fellow earns. The advantage of fellowships and research assistantships is that you kill two birds with one stone: you're being paid to do research, which is typically a requirement (if not the *primary* requirement) for your advanced degree.

> **Graduate students have three additional sources of funding to tap: fellowships, research assistantships, and ships.**

A word on choosing a graduate school. In Trap 3, I argued it's the student, not the college, that makes the biggest difference. Well, in the realm of graduate training, the rank of the school seems to matter more. If two people have graduate degrees from Harvard Business School, nobody cares that one of them did his undergraduate work at a no-name school. More is at stake when you've got MA or PhD or JD next to your name, since you're competing in a smaller but more lucrative job market.

My friend Nick wanted to go back for his MBA a few years after finishing his undergraduate program. He applied to several places, all of which rejected him. He hadn't applied to a safety school. Nick figured it wasn't worth spending the time and money to get his MBA unless he got into a top-notch university. So he stayed in the workforce, improved his GMAT score and earned stronger recommendation letters. Two years later, he was accepted into a prestigious MBA program, which really launched his career. Not a bad way to do it, since the money came out of his pocket.

The Bottom Line

Paying off your debts can seem overwhelming, but a strategy, a budget, and resolve go a long way toward making it happen. Moving back home is usually a huge cost saver, but make sure it doesn't ruin your relationships or facilitate a retreat into adolescence. Contribute to the family's expenses and assume the role of an adult in transition.

When you do leave home, keep your biggest expense — your living costs — under control so that you have enough money at the end of the month to make your loan payments and build up an emergency reserve. Stretch your dollars by shopping around for necessities, watching what you spend on food, increasing your W-4 allowances to take home more pay, never leasing a car, signing up for your company's full 401(k) match, and paying all your bills in full every month (including your loans). Beyond that, think about allocating any extra money toward paying off your loans faster or growing your savings. There's a place for both, but I generally favor loan reduction over long-term savings beyond your 401(k), as we saw in the story of Emily and Alexis.

Getting out of debt is not rocket science; it just takes a plan, and then lots of grit, determination, and consistency. Circumstances vary dramatically. Emily didn't need to pick up a second job or freelance; you might. Emily didn't need to live at home for a while; you might. Emily didn't need to go with an extended loan repayment plan; you might. But ignorance is the only excuse for defaulting on your student loans. And lack of commitment is the only reason you can't get on the path to financial freedom. With God's help, choose today to write the script of a debt-free future.

CONCLUSION

BE FREE FROM STUDENT DEBT SO YOU CAN LIVE WITH IMPACT

Congratulations! You now know more about paying for college, minimizing debt, and how to get out of debt than almost all the twenty-some million college students in this country. We've talked a lot about how to beat the college debt trap. Let's end with a few reflections on *why*. I'll give you three reasons, and then the ultimate reason.

Freedom to Choose Work You Love

Tragically, too many teachers, social workers, pastors, and others in lower-paying jobs today are struggling with student debt throughout their twenties, thirties, and even beyond. And many of you, afraid of such a future, are, for financial reasons, opting out of the work God made you to do. That's the wrong response. These are noble lines of work, important in our communities and honoring to God, that simply don't pay as well as other jobs. The right response is for future teachers, social workers, pastors, and others like them to *spend and borrow less for college* by employing the principles in this book. Freedom from student debt means freedom to choose the work you love without the pressure to come up with an extra several hundred dollars every month for the next decade or more.

Peace of Mind

Many college graduates lack peace of mind because they don't know how they're going to make their student debt payments. Their anxiety leads to sleeping problems, poor eating habits, and all kinds of relational dysfunction. It's one thing if your debt payments are small relative to a stable source of income. But when your debt load is high and you're unemployed or underemployed, it's as if there's a black cloud constantly hanging over your head. Freedom from student debt promotes peace of mind because it means there are fewer bills to pay and no debt collectors chasing you.

Preparation for Marriage

As I said in Trap 9, having debt doesn't disqualify you from marriage. What matters is if you're moving in the direction of living within your means and paying off your debt. But arguments about money are a frequent trigger for divorce. While financial problems can arise after marriage, bringing student debt into marriage is especially messy because it's *individual* debt—*his* debt or *her* debt, not *your* debt. If Tyler brings in $15,000 of debt, and Brianna brings in $35,000, it's easy for Tyler to become resentful or suspicious toward his bride. Theoretically, Tyler and Brianna both know "they" have $50,000 in debt, but it's not always easy to remember that fact when Brianna wants a $900 sofa and Tyler wants a $900 flat-screen TV. Freedom from student debt means bringing a clean financial slate into your marriage—an excellent gift to your future bride or groom.

The Ultimate Benefit:
Freedom to Advance God's Agenda

To understand the *ultimate* benefit of beating the college debt trap, let's examine one of the most bizarre parables Jesus ever told. We find it in chapter 16 of Luke's gospel. It's a story known as "the parable of the shrewd manager."

Mr. Shrewd Manager, let's call him Zach, works for a rich man,

whom we'll call Ryan. Ryan finds out that Zach is wasting money—
Ryan's money. Naturally, he's troubled. So he calls him in. "Hey,
Zach, I understand you've been irresponsible with my money." Zach
doesn't even try defending himself. He knows it's over. Ryan gives
him until the end of the day to clean out his office and hit the road.

Zach comes up with a brilliant plan. Ryan is a banker; lots of
people owe him money. Until 5:00 p.m., Zach still has the authority
to sign paperwork on Ryan's behalf. So Zach calls a bunch of the
people who owe Ryan money. He offers each of them an immediate 20 to 50 percent discount on their debt if they quickly sign the
paperwork. Sure enough, they come flocking in. And at 5:00 p.m.,
Zach heads for the door with a slew of new friends ready to scratch
his back the way he just scratched theirs.

Devious, isn't it? Zach was supposed to take care of Ryan's interests. It's hard to imagine it was in Ryan's best interest to forfeit what
scholars estimate would have been a year and a half's worth of wages
(Luke 16:4–7).[1] But what's so bizarre is that the master praises Zach
as he's heading home. Then Jesus seems to tell his disciples to go
and do likewise (verse 9). What in the world?

Jesus isn't praising Zach's sneaky trick. He's telling us to imitate
Zach in using money strategically to prepare for the future. We're
told, "For the people of this world are more shrewd in dealing with
their own kind than are the people of the light" (verse 8). People of
this world are often smarter in the ways of the world than Christians
are in the ways of God. People like Zach do a great job of using *their*
money to advance *their* agenda. Shouldn't we be as resourceful about
using *God's* money to advance *God's* agenda?

Everything we have is on loan from God: "The earth is the
LORD's and everything in it" (Psalm 24:1 NLT). When we get out
of debt, we honor God because we're displaying integrity by paying
back what we owe (Romans 13:7–8). Avoiding debt in the first place
means *not* having to pay Uncle Sam and Sallie Mae interest. It means
having more money to advance God's interests.

● ● ●

Though I've warned you about the traps to avoid, fundamentally this book's message is one of hope. Getting a college degree in something you enjoy and can master is entirely possible. You don't need to believe the hype that college is too expensive. You just need to understand how the system works and then work the system, apply yourself, and live within your means.

Beating the college debt trap lays the foundation for honoring God with money for a lifetime. It's not about getting rich so you can sit on a beach in the Bahamas and order cocktails. Wealth isn't the goal; freedom to serve God is. Those who don't have to send monthly checks to Sallie Mae have the freedom to put their efforts and earnings to work around the globe relieving suffering, lifting people out of extreme poverty, and sharing the saving message of Jesus Christ — making friends who will join them for eternity (Luke 16:9).

ACKNOWLEDGMENTS

Where to start? So many people helped make this book a reality. I'm grateful for Zondervan's partnership, especially for Carolyn McCready and Bridget Harmon. Carolyn, thanks for your confidence in this project from the beginning and your efforts to get my proposal approved. Bridget, thanks for your helpful correspondences along the way and for your help in securing research material.

Liz Heaney's editorial insight was invaluable in helping this manuscript reach its potential. And I'm beyond grateful to former students and other friends who took the time to read the chapters and provide substantive feedback. Thank you, Denise Astuto, Kellie Carstensen, Sabrina Cruz, Stephanie Dennis, Joey Esquibel, Jordan Gray, Kit Joos, Bobby Magby, Andy Naselli, Gina Rhue, Daniel Young, and Ken Young. My apologies to any others I accidentally omitted.

I'm thankful for higher education and debt repayment experts who graciously took the time to correspond with me, including Zac Bissonnette, Reyna Gobel, Anya Kamenetz, Mark Kantrowitz, and Lynn O'Shaughnessy. I've learned so much from your articles and books and from our interactions.

Finally, I must profusely thank my amazing wife, Marni, who once again read the entire manuscript, performed countless research dives, and bore with me in endless discussions about the issues in this book.

APPENDIX 1
EIGHT TAKEAWAYS YOU DON'T WANT TO MISS

1. A bachelor's degree is one of several options that can lead to a rewarding career. Before sleepwalking into a four-year college, make sure an associate's degree or enrolling in a trade school isn't a better fit for your talents and interests.

2. Being an informed customer is the best way to avoid spending a fortune on your education. Student loans should be a last resort, preferably limited to the last year or two of college, when you know you're in the right major and graduation is clearly in sight.

3. When considering colleges, stick with a budget—the way you would when shopping for anything else. Consider what it will cost you, not just for one year, but all the way through graduation. Research the college's financial aid track record for students in your income bracket. Look for value—financial aid generosity and instructional quality. Don't pay a fortune for prestige.

4. The phrase "financial aid" is nebulous. It can refer to grants (need-based gifts), scholarships (merit-based; you must work to maintain), work-study (a job that pays hourly), or loans (which you'll have to repay with interest). That's why collegedata.com is a great site. It breaks down financial aid by category. Net price (list price minus scholarships and grants) is what matters. Work-study is great because what you earn doesn't raise your expected family contribution for the next year.

5. Choose a major that's consistent with your interests and talents, but be mindful of your earnings prospects, particularly if you take out loans.

6. It *is* possible to earn most of the money you'll need for college while you're in college. It requires working hard, especially when classes are out of session, and working smart—leveraging your skills, taking on internships and other kinds of strategic employment, and minimizing your expenses through planning and discipline.

7. Start looking for a full-time job in advance of graduation. Prioritize identity capital in your search. Network, research your industry, and communicate clearly—always speaking to the *employer's* interests—on your résumé, cover letter, and interview.

8. Watch your housing and food expenses after you graduate. Free up enough cash to make your student loan payments on time. Build a reserve of short-term savings so that unexpected expenses don't kick you into credit card debt. As soon as possible, start throwing extra money at your loans to get out of debt faster (and save money by paying less interest).

APPENDIX 2

TWELVE BOOKS TO HELP YOU LEARN MORE

1. Acuff, Jon. *Quitter* (Brentwood, TN: Lampo, 2011).

2. Alcorn, Randy. *Money, Possessions, and Eternity* (Carol Stream, IL: Tyndale, 2003).

3. Bissonnette, Zac. *Debt-Free U* (New York: Portfolio Trade, 2010).

4. Chediak, Alex. *Thriving at College* (Carol Stream, IL: Tyndale, 2011).

5. Gobel, Reyna. *CliffsNotes Graduation Debt* (New York: Houghton Mifflin Harcourt, 2014).

6. Kantrowitz, Mark, and David Levy. *Filing the FAFSA* (Las Vegas, NV: Edvisors Network, 2013–2015).

7. Jay, Meg. *The Defining Decade* (New York: Hachette, 2012).

8. Newport, Cal. *So Good They Can't Ignore You* (New York: Hachette, 2012).

9. O'Shaughnessy, Lynn. *The College Solution*, 2nd ed. (Upper Saddle River, NJ: FT Press, 2012).

10. Pollak, Lindsey. *Getting from College to Career* (New York: Harper, 2012).

11. Ramsey, Dave. *The Total Money Makeover* (Nashville: Nelson, 2013).

12. Silva, Kenny. *Launch Your Life* (Nashville: Nelson, 2013).

NOTES

Introduction: Take Ownership of Your Financial Future

1. Some may point out that Emily should not feel obliged to tithe under these circumstances. That may be; the convictions of Christians differ on this matter. The point is that Emily was acting in accordance with her conscience—which all Christians would agree is commendable. For a summary of popular Christian views regarding tithing, see David A. Croteau, *Perspectives on Tithing: Four Views* (Nashville: Broadman & Holman, 2011).

2. Phil Izzo, "Congratulations to Class of 2014, Most Indebted Ever," *Wall Street Journal*, May 16, 2014, http://blogs.wsj.com/numbers/congratulations-to-class-of-2014-the-most-indebted-ever-1368/ (accessed March 26, 2015). Also, the Project on Student Debt—an initiative of The Institute for College Access & Success, releases average student debt data annually (see www.projectonstudentdebt.org).

3. "How America Pays for College 2013: Sallie Mae's National Study of College Students and Parents," 27, http://news.salliemae.com/research-tools/america-pays_2013 (accessed March 26, 2015).

4. "Voice of the Graduate," McKinsey & Company, in collaboration with Chegg, Inc., May 2013, http://mckinseyonsociety.com/voice-of-the-graduate (accessed March 26, 2015).

5. On both Perkins loans and *subsidized* Federal Stafford loans, Uncle Sam pays the interest as long as you're in school at least half-time. These loans can only be obtained by families with demonstrated financial need. More about this in Trap 5.

6. "Job Prospects, Health Insurance, and Student Loans Are Big Worries for College Students and Grads in 2012," eHealthInsurance, May 16, 2012, http://news.ehealthinsurance.com/news/job-prospects-health-insurance-234037 (accessed March 26, 2015).

7. "Pathways to Prosperity: Meeting the Challenge of Preparing Young Americans for the 21st Century," Harvard Graduate School of Education, February 11, 2011, www.gse.harvard.edu/news/11/02/pathways-prosperity-meeting-challenge-preparing-young-americans-21st-century (accessed March 26, 2015).

8. "U.S. Bankruptcy Courts—Business and Nonbusiness Cases Commenced, by Chapter of the Bankruptcy Code, during the 12-Month

Period Ending December 31, 2013," www.uscourts.gov/uscourts/
Statistics/BankruptcyStatistics/BankruptcyFilings/2013/1213_f2.pdf
(accessed March 25, 2015).

9. "Consumer Debt Statistics," Consolidated Credit Counseling Services,
www.consolidatedcredit.org/credit-card-debt/consumer-debt-facts/#back
(accessed March 26, 2015).

10. Douglas Belkin, "Parents Shell Out Less for Kids in College," *Wall Street
Journal*, July 23, 2013, www.wsj.com/articles/SB10001424127887324144
304578622343932131354 (accessed March 25, 2015). Belkin writes, "In
2013, 57% of families reported a student living at home or with a relative,
up from 43% three years ago."

Trap 1: Everyone Must Go to a Four-Year College

1. Anthony P. Carnevale, Tamara Jayasundera, and Andrew R. Hanson,
*Career and Technical Education: Five Ways That Pay Along the Way to the
B.A.* (Washington, D.C.: Georgetown University Center on Education
and the Workforce, 2012), 1, https://cew.georgetown.edu/report/career
-and-technical-education/ (accessed April 7, 2015).

2. The 65 to 70 percent figure includes enrollment in two-year schools
(data from "College Enrollment and Work Activity of High School
Graduates," Bureau of Labor Statistics, released annually; see Archived
News Releases, www.bls.gov/schedule/archives/all_nr.htm [accessed
April 15, 2015]).

3. Full-time enrollment in degree-granting institutions rose by 80 percent
from 1980 to 2010 ("Table 214: Total undergraduate fall enrollment in
degree-granting institutions, by attendance status, sex of student, and
control of institution: 1967 through 2010," National Center for Education
Statistics, http://nces.ed.gov/programs/digest/d11/tables/dt11_214.asp
[accessed March 25, 2015]). For the same period, there was a 47 percent
increase in the number of four-year colleges ("Table 306: Degree-
granting institutions, by control and level of institution: Selected years,
1949–50 through 2011–12," National Center for Education Statistics,
http://nces.ed.gov/programs/digest/d12/tables/dt12_306.asp [accessed
March 25, 2015]).

4. Almost all community colleges have an open admission policy, but just
because you're accepted doesn't mean you can get the classes you want.
Students are wait-listed when the classes they want to take are full. A
student could also be accepted on the condition that he or she first take
remedial level coursework.

5. Jeffrey J. Selingo, *College Unbound* (New York: New Harvest, 2013), 212.

6. Doug Lederman and Scott Jaschik, "Federal Accountability and
Financial Pressure: A Survey of Presidents" *Inside Higher Ed*,

March 7, 2014. http://www.insidehighered.com/news/survey/federal
-accountability-and-financial-pressure-survey-presidents.

7. According to the College Board (https://bigfuture.collegeboard.org/
college-search), as I write, one in six four-year colleges accepts "almost
all" applicants. Another one in six accepts "over 75 percent" of their
applicants. I'm not saying these colleges necessarily provide a bad
education; I'm just saying that acceptance into one of these colleges may
not be the accomplishment that acceptance to college was, say, in 1960.

8. Frank A. Brock, *An Educated Choice* (Phillipsburg, NJ: P&R, 2002), 33.

9. "Pathways to Prosperity: Meeting the Challenge of Preparing Young
Americans for the 21st Century," Harvard Graduate School of Education,
February 2011, www.gse.harvard.edu/news/11/02/pathways-prosperity
-meeting-challenge-preparing-young-americans-21st-century (accessed
March 26, 2015).

10. "The Toolbox Revisited: Paths to Degree Completion from High School
through College," February 2006, U.S. Department of Education,
www2.ed.gov/rschstat/research/pubs/toolboxrevisit/toolbox.pdf, 35 – 36
(accessed March 25, 2015).

11. The precise figure is 35 percent. See "Time Is the Enemy," September
2011, 14, Complete College America, www.completecollege.org/docs/
Time_Is_the_Enemy.pdf (accessed April 7, 2015).

12. Sociologist James E. Rosenbaum, who studied this extensively, has
concluded that a student's chance of success in college is "highly
predicted" from their high school grades. See James Rosenbaum, *Beyond
College for All: Career Paths for the Forgotten Half* (New York: Russell Sage
Foundation, 2001), 55 – 87.

13. "Family Income and Education Attainment, 1970 to 2009," *Postsecondary
Education Opportunity*, February 2012, www.postsecondary.org/
last12/221_1110pg1_16.pdf (accessed April 7, 2015).

14. Data from the Bureau of Labor Statistics, "College Enrollment and Work
Activity of High School Graduates" (released annually); "Pathways to
Prosperity Project," Harvard Graduate School of Education, February
2011, 10; U.S. Census Bureau, "Statistical Abstract of the U.S. 2013,"
Table 236, Educational Attainment by Selected Characteristics: 2012.

15. With subsidized loans, Uncle Sam picks up your interest as long as you're
a full-time student. But the annual cap on those is not high enough to
cover most of the bill.

16. "Fast Facts: Back to School Statistics 2014," National Center for
Education Statistics, http://nces.ed.gov/fastfacts/display.asp?id=372
(accessed April 7, 2015).

17. Jeff Guo, "Attention college students: You may have earned a degree
without knowing it," *Washington Post*, February 10, 2015, www.washington
post.com/blogs/govbeat/wp/2015/02/10/attention-college-students-you
-may-have-earned-a-degree-without-knowing-it (accessed April 9, 2015).

18. Anthony P. Carnevale, Nicole Smith, and Jeff Strohl, *Help Wanted: Projections of Jobs and Education Requirements Through 2018* (Washington, D.C.: Georgetown University Center on Education and the Workforce, 2010), https://cew.georgetown.edu/report/help-wanted/ (accessed April 9, 2015).

19. Scott A. Ginder and Janice E. Kelly-Reid, "Postsecondary Institutions and Cost of Attendance in 2012–13; Degrees and Other Awards Conferred, 2011–12; and 12-Month Enrollment, 2011–12," National Center for Education Statistics, Table 3, http://nces.ed.gov/pubs2013/2013289rev.pdf (accessed April 7, 2015).

20. See the list of fastest-growing occupations from the Bureau of Labor Statistics, www.bls.gov/emp/ep_table_103.htm (accessed April 7, 2015).

21. Occupation-specific figures are according to the Bureau of Labor Statistics (BLS), "Occupational Employment Statistics" (www.bls.gov/oes/home.htm), as of May 2012. As I write, the latest available average salary figure of a person whose highest degree is a bachelor's is for 2011 ($59,415); see "Census Bureau Reports Fast Growth in PhDs and Master's Degree Holders," January 23, 2013, U.S. Census Bureau, www.census.gov/newsroom/press-releases/2013/cb13-13.html (accessed April 7, 2015). Based on the increase from 2009 to 2011, I extrapolated the 2012 salary figure for a person with a bachelor's degree to be approximately $61,000.

22. Carnevale, Smith, and Strohl, *Help Wanted*.

23. CollegeMeasures.org has been publishing this data on their website. As I write, data is available for Texas, Virginia, Arkansas, Tennessee, Colorado, and Florida. They hope to add data for other states in the future.

24. Summary reports for Texas, Colorado, Virginia, and Tennessee can be accessed at http://collegemeasures.org/category/Reports---ESM.aspx?page=2 (accessed April 7, 2015).

25. Anthony P. Carnevale, Stephen J. Rose, and Ban Cheah, *The College Payoff: Education, Occupations, Lifetime Earnings* (Washington, D.C.: Georgetown University Center on Education and the Workforce, 2011), 3, https://georgetown.app.box.com/s/cwmx7i5li1nxd7zt7mim (accessed April 7, 2015).

26. "2013 Talent Shortage Survey Research Results," Manpower Group, 39, www.manpowergroup.us/campaigns/talent-shortage-2013/pdf/2013_Talent_Shortage_Survey_Results_US_lo_0510.pdf (accessed April 7, 2015).

27. "2012 Talent Shortage Survey Research Results," Manpower Group, 5. www.manpowergroup.us/campaigns/talent-shortage-2012/pdf/2012_Talent_Shortage_Survey_Results_US_FINALFINAL.pdf (accessed April 7, 2015).

28. Some trade schools grant a highly marketable Associate of Applied Sciences (AAS) degree at the completion of their training.

29. Joshua Wright, "America's Skilled Trades Dilemma: Shortages Loom as Most-In-Demand Group of Workers Ages," *Forbes*, March 7, 2013, www .forbes.com/sites/emsi/2013/03/07/americas-skilled-trades-dilemma -shortages-loom-as-most-in-demand-group-of-workers-ages/ (accessed April 7, 2015).

30. Carnevale, Jayasundera, and Hanson, *Career and Technical Education*, 22–26, https://cew.georgetown.edu/report/career-and-technical -education/ (accessed April 7, 2015).

31. If you don't, it's easy to lose your study skills/habits and flounder if and when you do go to college.

32. A number of explicitly Christian gap-year programs are listed at www .cpyu.org/gapyear. Some feature a mix of apologetics, evangelism, and missions; others focus on personal discipleship, theological training, and life skills development in the context of community.

Trap 2: It's All Just Going to Work Out

1. Scott Cohn, "Occupy Wall Street Protesters Demand Student Loan Relief," October 12, 2011, CNBC.com, www.cnbc.com/id/44879455 (accessed April 7, 2015).

2. "We Are the 99 Percent," November 4, 2011, http://wearethe99percent .tumblr.com/post/12324810536/i-am-24-years-old-and-am-90-000-in-debt -from (accessed April 9, 2015). The name is fictional.

3. For enrollment data, see "Digest of Education Statistics," Table 214: "Total undergraduate fall enrollment in degree-granting institutions, by attendance status, sex of student, and control of institution: 1967 through 2010," National Center for Education Statistics, http://nces.ed.gov/ programs/digest/d11/tables/dt11_214.asp (accessed April 9, 2015). Even after adjusting for inflation, the total cost of instruction at a four-year college more than doubled from 1980 to 2010 at both public and private institutions (see "Fast Facts: Tuition costs of colleges and universities," National Center for Education Statistics, http://nces.ed.gov/fastfacts/ display.asp?id=76 [accessed April 9, 2015]).

4. "Education Pays 2010: The Benefits of Higher Education for Individuals and Society," College Board Advocacy & Policy Center, 17, 20, http:// trends.collegeboard.org/sites/default/files/education-pays-2010-full -report.pdf (accessed April 9, 2015).

5. See Katherine Peralta, "College Grads Taking Low-Wage Jobs Displace Less Educated," *Bloomberg*, March 12, 2014, www.bloomberg.com/news/ articles/2014-03-06/college-grads-taking-low-wage-jobs-displace-less -educated (accessed April 9, 2015).

6. See Paul Abrahamson, "2014 College Construction Report," *College Planning and Management*, February 2014, 20–28, http://pdf.101com

.com/CPMmag/2014/FEB.pdf (accessed April 9, 2015); see also Paul
Abrahamson, "2014 College Housing Report," May 2014, *College Planning
and Management*, 20–31, www.mahlum.com/pdf/CPM2014College
HousingReport%281%29.pdf (accessed April 9, 2015).

7. See Abrahamson, "2014 College Housing Report," May 2014, *College
Planning and Management*, 26.

8. Mark J. Perry, "Today's new homes are 1,000 square feet larger than
in 1973, and the living space per person has doubled over last 40
years," *American Enterprise Institute*, February 26, 2014, www.aei-ideas
.org/2014/02/todays-new-homes-are-1000-square-feet-larger-than-in
-1973-and-the-living-space-per-person-has-doubled-over-last-40-years
(accessed April 15, 2015).

9. Jay P. Greene, "Administrative Bloat at American Universities: The
Real Reason for High Costs in Higher Education," Goldwater Institute
Policy Report, no. 239, August 17, 2010, 1, www.goldwaterinstitute.org/
en/work/topics/education/education-spending/administrative-bloat-at-
american-universities-the-/ (accessed April 15, 2015). It's fair to point
out, however, that some of the administrative growth is associated with
expanding accreditation requirements and government regulations.

10. The University of California system (where I did my graduate studies) is
infamous in this regard. In the fall of 2012, when they faced the threat of
$250 million in additional state funding cuts (on top of $1 billion in cuts
since 2007), UC San Diego hired its first-ever vice chancellor for equity,
diversity, and inclusion—at a starting salary of $250,000, a relocation
allowance of $60,000, and a temporary housing allowance of $13,500.
All this while UC tuition was escalating and course offerings were
being slashed. See Heather Mac Donald, "Multiculti U," *City Journal*,
vol. 23, no. 2, Spring 2013, www.city-journal.org/2013/23_2_multiculti
-university.html (accessed April 15, 2015).

11. Sallie Mae and Ipsos produce an annual report on how Americans
pay for college. See the 2014 report, "How America Pays for
College 2014: Sallie Mae's National Study of College Students
and Parents," at http://news.salliemae.com/files/doc_library/file/
HowAmericaPaysforCollege2014FNL.pdf (accessed April 15, 2015).

12. State and federal grants give funds directly to students rather than to the
public universities.

13. See Andrew Martin and Andrew W. Lehren, "A Generation Hobbled
by the Soaring Cost of College," *New York Times*, May 12, 2012, www
.nytimes.com/2012/05/13/business/student-loans-weighing-down-a
-generation-with-heavy-debt.html (accessed April 15, 2015).

14. Phil Izzo, "Number of the Week: Class of 2013, Most Indebted Ever,"
Wall Street Journal, May 18, 2013, http://blogs.wsj.com/economics/
2013/05/18/number-of-the-week-class-of-2013-most-indebted-ever/
(accessed April 15, 2015).

15. There's surprising agreement on this issue from those on the political left and right. See, for example, Robert Samuels, *Why Public Higher Education Should Be Free* (New Brunswick, NJ: Rutgers University Press, 2013); William J. Bennett and David Wilezol, *Is College Worth It?* (Nashville: Nelson, 2013). Samuels is a progressive (liberal), while Bennett and Wilezol are conservatives. These authors differ on issues related to higher education policy, but both books argue that student loans are contributing to the unaffordability of college.

16. The underwriting fee could also represent the cost to an investor who will subsequently repurchase your loan.

17. Some colleges use the Federal Need Analysis Methodology, and others rely on an Institutional Methodology established by the College Board. The latter takes into account a wider range of assets, such as home equity.

18. The sticker price (a.k.a., total cost of instruction) is not irrelevant. A higher number *can* be indicative of higher quality instructional resources (better laboratories, classrooms, and so on). It could also mean they spend a ton on campus amenities. We'll come back to this in Trap 3.

19. Private loans *do* involve a credit check. Since many college students have little to no credit history, lenders offer better terms on private loans if parents cosign. But cosigning presents risk for your parents, and there are many reasons to avoid private loans entirely.

Trap 3: Spend a Fortune on Prestige (and Other Bad Ideas)

1. Anthony P. Carnevale, Tamara Jayasundara, and Andrew R. Hanson, *Career and Technical Education: Five Ways That Pay Along the Way to the B.A.* (Washington, D.C.: Georgetown University Center on Education and the Workforce, 2012), 1, https://cew.georgetown.edu/report/career-and-technical-education/ (accessed April 9, 2015).

2. I assumed a 5 percent interest rate and a 1 percent origination fee. I used the loan calculator at www.finaid.org.

3. I've written a chapter about it in another book (*Preparing Your Teens for College* [Carol Stream, IL: Tyndale, 2014]). In chapter 10, I addressed academic, professional, spiritual, and other factors worth considering.

4. See Leigh Jones, "Default Position," *World*, April 20, 2013, www.worldmag.com/2013/04/default_position (accessed April 15, 2015).

5. Andrew Martin and Andrew W. Lehren, "A Generation Hobbled by the Soaring Cost of College," *New York Times*, May 12, 2012, www.nytimes.com/2012/05/13/business/student-loans-weighing-down-a-generation-with-heavy-debt.html (accessed April 15, 2015).

6. See Mark Kantrowitz, "Debt at Graduation," Edvisors Network, January 7, 2014, 5–6, www.edvisors.com/media/files/student-aid-policy/20140107-debt-at-graduation.pdf (accessed April 15, 2015). Those

who borrow incredibly large sums of money "pull up" the average level of indebtedness.

7. See William G. Bowen, Matthew M. Chingos, and Michael S. McPherson, *Crossing the Finish Line* (Princeton, NJ: Princeton University Press, 2009), 87–112.

8. For a real-world example, see Lynn O'Shaughnessy's July 24, 2013, post "Beware of the College Bait and Switch," www.thecollegesolution .com/beware-of-the-college-bait-and-switch (accessed April 15, 2015). O'Shaughnessy is a great resource for mining the treasures of Collegedata.com.

9. See Stacy Berg Dale and Alan B. Krueger, "Estimating the Payoff to Attending a More Selective College: An Application of Selection on Observables and Unobservables," *Quarterly Journal of Economics*, November 2002, 1491–1527. Consistent with the conclusion of Bowen, Chingos, and McPherson (see note 7 above), Dale and Krueger found that students from "disadvantageous backgrounds ... benefit most from attending a more elite college."

10. The sample size was two thousand college students and one thousand hiring managers (see "Bridge That Gap: Analyzing the Student Skill Index," Chegg, Inc., Fall 2013, www.insidehighered.com/sites/default/ server_files/files/Bridge%20That%20Gap-v8.pdf [accessed April 15, 2015]).

11. Malcolm Gladwell, *David and Goliath: Underdogs, Misfits, and the Art of Battling Giants* (New York: Little, Brown and Company), 2013, chapter 3. Gladwell notes that these SAT figures are several years old and cites original research sources.

12. As I write, the latest figures are for 2013 (see www.payscale.com/college -education-value-2013 [accessed April 15, 2015]). For the details of PayScale's methodology, go to www.payscale.com/data-packages/college -roi-2013/methodology (accessed April 15, 2015).

13. Data from all fifty states is, in principle, available because states can link data "that document each student's experiences (e.g., major field of study) to unemployment-insurance records that track post-college earnings and field of employment" (Mark Schneider, "States Have an Opportunity to Inform Colleges and Students," *The Chronicle of Higher Education*, October 22, 2012, http://chronicle.com/article/States-Have-an -Opportunity-to/135218 [accessed April 15, 2015]). But as I write, these kinds of proposals are stuck in Congress due to privacy concerns.

14. For example, former Yale professor William Deresiewicz has observed that as of 2010, about a third of graduates from top schools like Harvard, Princeton, and Cornell went into financing and consulting—professions that pay handsomely (see William Deresiewicz, "Don't Send Your Kid to the Ivy League," *New Republic*, July 21, 2014, www.newrepublic.com/ article/118747/ivy-league-schools-are-overrated-send-your-kids-elsewhere [accessed April 15, 2015]).

15. Stacy Berg Dale and Alan B. Krueger, "Estimating the Payoff to Attending a More Selective College: An Application of Selection on Observables and Unobservables," *Quarterly Journal of Economics*, November 2002, 1491–1527.

16. Figures are from the National Center for Education Statistics (NCES) College Navigator (http://nces.ed.gov/collegenavigator [accessed April 15, 2015]).

17. *Unless* the students came from low-income families. Then, those who picked U Penn did better. This is consistent with my earlier statements about the benefits of selective universities for low-income students (assuming these students aren't asked to take on hefty debt loads).

18. A recent book that makes this point well and provides a wide variety of examples is Frank Bruni, *Where You Go Is Not Who You'll Be: An Antidote to the College Admissions Mania* (New York: Hachette, 2015).

19. CSS stands for College Scholarship Service.

20. The College Board's website (bigfuture.org) has a good EFC calculator.

21. Take, for example, The Great Books Honors College at Faulkner University (studyliberalarts.org) and LibertasU (libertasu.com).

22. See Thomas K. Lindsay, "Anatomy of a Revolution? The Rise of the $10,000 Bachelor's Degree," Texas Public Policy Foundation, September 2012, www.texaspolicy.com/sites/default/files/documents/2012-09-RR07 -AnatomyOfARevolution10000Degree-CHE-TomLindsay.pdf (accessed April 15, 2015); Arthur C. Brooks, "My Valuable, Cheap College Degree," *New York Times*, January 31, 2013, www.nytimes.com/2013/02/01/opinion/ my-valuable-cheap-college-degree.html (accessed April 15, 2015). Brooks followed his $10K-BA with an inexpensive MA and PhD. He went on to become a tenured professor at Syracuse University.

23. I. Elaine Allen and Jeff Seaman, "Going the Distance: Online Education in the United States, 2011," Babson Survey Research Group, 4, www .onlinelearningsurvey.com/reports/goingthedistance.pdf (accessed April 15, 2015).

Trap 4: Choose Your Major on a Whim

1. The precise reported figure is 35 percent. See "Time Is the Enemy," Complete College America, September 2011, 14, www.completecollege .org/docs/Time_Is_the_Enemy.pdf (accessed April 15, 2015).

2. John H. Pryor et al., "The American Freshman: National Norms Fall 2012" (Los Angeles: Higher Education Research Institute, UCLA, 2012), www.heri.ucla.edu/monographs/theamericanfreshman2012.pdf (accessed April 15, 2015).

3. See "Voice of the Graduate," McKinsey & Company, in collaboration with Chegg, Inc., May 2013, http://mckinseyonsociety.com/voice-of-the -graduate (accessed April 15, 2015).

4. See Anthony Carnevale, Ban Cheah, and Jeff Strohl, "Hard Times 2013: College Majors, Unemployment and Earnings," Georgetown University Center on Education and the Workforce, May 2013, https:// cew.georgetown.edu/report/hard-times (accessed April 15, 2015).

5. See "Digest of Education Statistics," Table 322.10, National Center for Education Statistics. In the 2011–2012 academic year, 81,382 bachelor degrees in engineering were granted, while 95,797 bachelor degrees in visual and performing arts were earned.

6. The research of Stuart Rojstaczer and Christopher Healy has demonstrated that college grades have risen in all subjects, but that average grades today in the humanities are higher than in the hard sciences and engineering (see Stuart Rojstaczer and Christopher Healy, "Grading in American Colleges and Universities," Teachers College Record, March 4, 2010), http://www.gradeinflation.com/tcr2010grading. pdf [accessed April 15, 2015]). Grade inflation is most prominent at elite private universities. It's least prominent at public universities in the STEM fields.

7. Jeffrey J. Selingo, *College (Un)bound* (New York: Houghton Mifflin Harcourt, 2013), 147.

8. See Peter Cappelli, "Why Focusing Too Narrowly in College Could Backfire," *Wall Street Journal*, November 15, 2013, www.wsj.com/articles/ SB10001424127887324139404579016662718868576 (accessed April 15, 2015).

9. Jordan Weissmann, "Money Is a Terrible Way to Measure the Value of a College Major," *The Atlantic*, January 23, 2014, www.theatlantic.com/ business/archive/2014/01/money-is-a-terrible-way-to-measure-the-value -of-a-college-major/283290 (accessed April 15, 2015).

10. See, for example, "Education or Reputation? A Look at America's Top-Ranked Liberal Arts Colleges," American Council of Trustees and Alumni, January 2014, www.goacta.org/images/download/education_or _reputation.pdf (accessed April 15, 2015).

11. See Carolyn Gregoire, "This Is Irrefutable Evidence of the Value of a Humanities Education," *Huffington Post*, January 28, 2014, www .huffingtonpost.com/2014/01/28/the-unusual-college-major_n_4654757 .html (accessed April 15, 2015); Steve Sadove, "Employees Who Stand Out," *Forbes*, September 5, 2014, www.forbes.com/sites/ realspin/2014/09/05/employees-who-stand-out (accessed April 15, 2015).

12. See "Bridge That Gap: Analyzing the Student Skill Index," Chegg, Inc., Fall 2013, www.insidehighered.com/sites/default/server_files/files/ Bridge%20That%20Gap-v8.pdf (accessed April 15, 2015).

13. See Philip Babcock and Mindy Marks, "Leisure College, USA," American Enterprise Institute for Public Policy Research, August 2010, www.econ.ucsb.edu/papers/wp02-10.pdf (accessed April 15, 2015). Similar data was presented in Richard Arum and Josipa Roksa, *Academically Adrift: Limited Learning on College Campuses* (Chicago: University of Chicago Press, 2011), 69. More positively, the 2013 National Survey of Student Engagement (NSSE), found that "in a typical week, first-year students averaged 14 hours and seniors averaged 15 hours preparing for class (studying, reading, writing, doing homework or lab work, etc.)." (National Survey of Student Engagement, Annual Results 2013, 9, http://nsse.iub.edu/NSSE_2013_Results [accessed April 15, 2015]).

14. See Arum and Roksa, *Academically Adrift*.

15. Richard Arum, coauthor of *Academically Adrift*, is quoted as expressing these sentiments in Jeffrey J. Selingo's *College (Un)bound*, 147–48.

16. Two thousand students and one thousand hiring managers were surveyed (see "Bridge That Gap," Chegg, Inc., Fall 2013).

17. Ibid.

18. An A- (3.67/4.00) is more impressive if the professor gave an average grade that semester of 3.00 rather than 3.50. It means you stood out from the pack that much more. Some colleges are now adding this kind of comparative information to student transcripts. I suspect others will follow suit in the years to come.

Trap 5: Student Loans Are Always Worth It

1. A small number of elite universities require that financial aid applicants complete the CSS/Financial Aid PROFILE. The PROFILE takes a deeper look at the financial assets of a dependent student's parents, such as their home equity. This method of financial aid determination is known as Institutional Methodology.

2. Other factors include whether you require child care for a dependent, whether you have a disability, and whether you're participating in a study-abroad program. For further details, see "Wondering how the amount of your federal student aid is determined," Federal Student Aid, https://studentaid.ed.gov/fafsa/next-steps/how-calculated (accessed April 15, 2015).

3. Technically, cost of attendance (COA) is the ceiling on *total financial aid*. Need-based and merit-based aid, combined, cannot exceed COA.

4. Some of the universities that claim to meet 100 percent of a student's demonstrated financial need are using the Institutional Methodology (IM) to determine a student's financial need. As I mentioned in Trap 3, the IM takes a deeper look at the resources of a student's family, such as home equity. The result is that a student "looks richer," which means he

or she has a *higher EFC* and ends up having *less* demonstrated financial need. The university is meeting 100 percent of this *lower* demonstrated financial need figure. Nevertheless, these universities are among the most generous in the country.

5. See Lynn O'Shaughnessy, *The College Solution*, 2nd ed. (Upper Saddle River, NJ: FT Press), 2012, 44–47.

6. Federal Stafford loans are often called Direct loans because the money is loaned to students directly by the U.S. Department of Education. I'm using the term Federal Stafford loans to avoid confusion, since Federal PLUS loans are also Direct loans.

7. Per the Bipartisan Student Loan Certainty Act of 2013 (enacted August 9, 2013), the interest rate of Direct loans (i.e., Federal Stafford loans and Federal PLUS loans) are tied to the ten-year Treasury note.

8. For details on how FAFSA determines your dependency status, see http://studentaid.ed.gov/fafsa/filling-out/dependency#dependent-or -independent. If you're classified as a dependent student, but your parents are unable to obtain Federal PLUS Loans, you may be eligible to take out unsubsidized Federal Stafford loans up to the higher limits associated with independent students. Inquire at your college.

9. These may change.

10. There's a limit on the time window in which you can receive a subsidized Federal Stafford loan. The maximum eligibility period is 150 percent of the published length of your program (three years for a two-year associate's degree and six years for a four-year bachelor's degree). The same limit applies toward Federal Pell Grant eligibility.

11. See Marian Wang, Beckie Supiano, and Andrea Fuller, "The Parent Loan Trap," *The Chronicle of Higher Education*, October 4, 2012, http://chronicle .com/article/The-Parent-Plus-Trap/134844 (accessed April 15, 2015).

12. They could pursue a cash-out refinance, a home equity loan, or a home equity line of credit. I would encourage anyone considering one of these options to prioritize a fixed, low interest rate and to keep their overall debt level considerably below the *current* market value of their home (not some optimistic *projected* value).

13. Fixed-rate private student loans are a relatively new phenomenon. About half of private student loan programs now offer fixed-rate options. The problem is, you still don't have the protections that come with federal loans, such as deferment and mandatory forbearance. If you're borrowing a small amount of money, have a reliable full-time job, and can get a low, fixed interest rate, a private loan becomes less of a concern.

14. See Mark Kantrowitz, "Debt at Graduation," Edvisors Network, January 7, 2014, www.edvisors.com/media/files/student-aid-policy/20140107-debt -at-graduation.pdf (accessed April 15, 2015).

15. It'd actually be a little more, as the interest figure (initially $250) would compound as the principal grew.

16. I estimate that $1,000 of interest accumulates on the $5,000 borrowed your first year, $750 in interest accumulates on the $5,000 borrowed your second year, then $500, and finally $250. That's $2,500 of capitalized interest added to the $20,000 borrowed for a total of $22,500. Add four origination fees of $50 each, and you get $22,700. Assume all the loans were taken out at a 5 percent interest rate, and you get a monthly payment of about $240.

17. I got this figure by estimating 15 percent for federal tax (about right for a new college graduate), 4 percent state tax, 6.2 percent for Social Security, and 1.45 percent for Medicare. The latter two are exact figures as of this writing. State taxes vary widely.

18. Unless you consolidate your federal loans, in which case you can get a repayment plan of up to thirty years, depending on your loan balance. If the loan balance is less than $7,500, the repayment term is ten years. If it's $7,500–$9,999, it's twelve years. If $10,000–$19,999, it's fifteen years. If $20,000–$39,999, it's twenty years. If $40,000–$59,999, it's twenty-five years. If more than $60,000, it's thirty years. We'll discuss the merits and demerits of loan consolidation in Trap 9.

19. The repayment term depends on the loan balance in the same manner as with consolidation under the Graduated Repayment Plan.

20. You must meet certain other requirements as well. Get the details from your loan servicer.

21. This program is known as the Public Service Loan Forgiveness (PSLF) Program. Details are available at https://studentaid.ed.gov/repay-loans/forgiveness-cancellation/charts/public-service.

22. You can also get a deferment in other kinds of extenuating circumstances, such as active duty military service during a war, a military operation, or a national emergency. If you're in a tough situation, it doesn't hurt to have a conversation with your loan servicer.

23. See the information at https://studentaid.ed.gov/repay-loans/deferment-forbearance#what-is-forbearance.

24. See Alisa F. Cunningham and Gregory S. Kienzl, "Delinquency: The Untold Story of Student Loan Borrowing," Institute for Higher Education Policy, March 2011, www.ihep.org/sites/default/files/uploads/docs/pubs/delinquency-the_untold_story_final_march_2011.pdf (accessed April 15, 2015).

25. Michael Stratford, "Default Rates Rise Again," *Inside Higher Ed*, October 1, 2013. More recent data suggest that default rates are slightly ticking down from the figures reported in 2013.

26. "New Data Confirm Troubling Student Loan Default Problems," The Institute for College Access & Success, September 30, 2013. http://projectonstudentdebt.org/files/pub/CDR_2013_NR.pdf.

Trap 6: I Can't Get Meaningful Work as a Student

1. From 2007 to 2012, the percentage of parents who believed they'd be able to help their children pay for college dropped from one in two to just one in four (see Kayla Webley, "Sorry, Kids: Your Parents Feel Less Able to Help Pay for College," *Time*, March 29, 2012, http://business.time.com/2012/03/29/sorry-kids-your-parents-feel-less-able-to-help-pay-for-college/ [accessed April 15, 2015]).

2. Twelve units is the minimum to be considered full-time. When I went to college as a full-time student, I was allowed to take *unlimited* units. I did a few twenty- to twenty-two-unit semesters and graduated early.

3. See Philip Babcock and Mindy Marks, "Leisure College, USA," American Enterprise Institute for Public Policy Research, August 2010, www.econ.ucsb.edu/papers/wp02-10.pdf (accessed April 15, 2015).

4. The $6,310 figure is for a dependent student using the 2015–2016 FAFSA formula guide, an increase of $50 over the 2014–2015 academic year. This amount (known as the *income protection allowance* or IPA) is greater for independent students. If you Google "EFC formula guide," you can find a PDF file that walks you through the formula for the current academic year.

5. This is a good reason to get your savings account to as close to zero as possible before you begin the financial aid process. If you're planning to buy things for college, do it before filing the FAFSA. You could even give whatever money is left to your parents. The FAFSA taxes your parents' savings much less than it taxes yours.

6. Not including whatever you end up paying in federal and state taxes.

7. Quoted in Zac Bissonnette, *Debt-Free U* (New York: Penguin, 2010), 216.

8. Surveying more than 4,900 former Chegg customers in October–November 2012, McKinsey & Company reported that "in searching for a job, most graduates report using a 'do it yourself' approach; the vast majority do not use career services offered by their college or tap into alumni networks to help find a job" ("Voice of the Graduate," McKinsey & Company, in collaboration with Chegg, Inc., May 2013, http://mckinseyonsociety.com/voice-of-the-graduate [accessed April 15, 2015]).

9. For an insightful book containing ninety tips on moving from college to career, see Lindsey Pollak, *Getting from College to Career: Your Essential Guide to Succeeding in the Real World* (New York: Harper, 2012).

10. "Average Published Undergraduate Charges by Sector, 2014–15," College Board: Trends in Higher Education, http://trends.collegeboard.org/college-pricing/figures-tables/average-published-undergraduate-charges-sector-2014-15 (accessed April 15, 2015).

Trap 7: I Can't Control My Expenses

1. This pithy quote is from Mark Kantrowitz.
2. In 2013, 57 percent of families reported a college student living at home or with a relative, up from 43 percent in 2010. Even among families with incomes greater than $100,000, the share of students staying at home in 2013 doubled to 48 percent since 2009–2010. See Douglas Belkin, "Parents Shell Out Less for Kids in College," *Wall Street Journal*, July 23, 2013, www.wsj.com/articles/SB100014241278873241443045786223439321 31354 (accessed April 15, 2015).
3. A semester is (at most) fifteen weeks, plus (at most) a week of finals. So let's say that two semesters is thirty-two weeks. On average there are 4.33 weeks per month (fifty-two weeks divided by twelve months), so thirty-two weeks converts to 7.38 months. The eight-month figure is generous. If a college is on the quarter system, they'll typically run ten-week quarters, and most students will take the summer quarter off. Two semesters is roughly the equivalent of three quarters.
4. As previously noted, a semester is (at most) fifteen weeks of instruction, plus one week of finals. Sixteen weeks is actually 3.7 months.
5. Senator Joseph R. Biden Jr., "Excessive Drinking on America's College Campuses," October 19, 2000, citing data from the National Center on Addiction and Substance Abuse (CASA) at Columbia University, "Rethinking Rites of Passage: Substance Abuse on America's Campuses," June 1994, 21, www.casacolumbia.org/addiction-research/ reports/rethinking-rites-of-passage-substance-abuse-americas-campuses (accessed April 15, 2015).
6. See Lewis D. Eigen, "Alcohol Practices, Policies, and Potentials of American Colleges and Universities," U.S. Dept. of Health and Human Services, September 1991, http://files.eric.ed.gov/fulltext/ED350928.pdf (accessed April 15, 2015). Though this study is dated, I'm not aware of any subsequent study that paints a different picture. Eigen wrote, "Each year, college students spend $5.5 billion on alcohol (mostly beer). This is more than they spend on books, soda, coffee, juice, and milk, combined. On a typical campus, the average amount a student spends annually on alcohol is $466." Eigen also reported that "nearly 7% of first-year students who drop out do so because of alcohol-related problems."
7. Lloyd D. Johnston et al, "Monitoring the Future National Survey Results on Drug Use, 1975–2012, vol. 2: College Students and Adults Ages 19–50," Institute for Social Research, University of Michigan, 2013.
8. Not including the Federal PLUS loan program, an option for your parents.
9. Zac Bissonnette, *Debt-Free U* (New York: Penguin, 2010), 243.
10. Perhaps far more than 10 percent, depending on how God prospers us. For a comprehensive book on money, see Randy Alcorn, *Money, Possessions, and Eternity* (Carol Stream, IL: Tyndale, 2003). For a helpful

study on what the Bible says about tithing and giving, see David A. Croteau, *Tithing after the Cross* (Gonzalez, FL: Energion, 2013).

11. I'm assuming a 10 percent interest rate.

12. According to the College Board, published tuition and fees for the 2014–2015 academic year were $9,139 at public, four-year, in-state institutions, which works out to almost $765 per month. Room and board were $9,804, or about $820 per month, which I divided into housing ($550) and food ($270). See "Average Net Price over Time for Full-Time Students at Four-Year Public Institutions," College Board: Trends in Higher Education, https://trends.collegeboard.org/college-pricing/figures-tables/average-net-price-full-time-students-over-time-public-institutions (accessed April 15, 2015).

13. Derek Thompson, "Yes, Credit Cards Are Making You a Bad Person," *The Atlantic*, June 12, 2013, www.theatlantic.com/business/archive/2013/06/yes-credit-cards-are-making-you-a-bad-person/276777 (accessed April 15, 2015).

14. There are exceptions—for example, gas stations that only accept cash or debit cards and have lower prices.

15. This is known as manual underwriting. See Dave Ramsey, "The Truth about Your Credit Score," June 11, 2010, www.daveramsey.com/article/the-truth-about-your-credit-score/lifeandmoney_creditcards?ictid=fpu_content (accessed April 15, 2015).

Trap 8: Finding a High-Paying Job Will Be a Breeze

1. David Smith, Katherine LaVelle, and Anthony Abbatiello, "Great Expectations: Insights from the Accenture 2014 College Graduate Employment Survey," Accenture Strategy, March 2014, www.accenture.com/SiteCollectionDocuments/PDF/Accenture-2014-College-Graduates-Survey.pdf (accessed April 15, 2015).

2. The 2013 survey I cited earlier—"Voice of the Graduate"—found that 45 percent of recent graduates were underemployed (McKinsey & Company, in collaboration with Chegg, Inc., May 2013, http://mckinseyonsociety.com/voice-of-the-graduate [accessed April 15, 2015]).

3. Meg Jay, *The Defining Decade: Why Your Twenties Matter—and How to Make the Most of Them Now* (New York: Hachette, 2013), 7. For illustrative purposes, I've embellished Jay's example of Helen (itself a composite).

4. The concept of career capital is one I picked up from Cal Newport's provocative book, *So Good They Can't Ignore You* (New York: Hachette, 2012).

5. My thinking about informational interviews has been influenced by Lindsey Pollak's insightful book, *Getting from College to Career*, rev. ed. (New York: HarperBusiness, 2012).

6. In the psychology literature, this has become known as the Ben Franklin effect. As the story goes, Franklin once asked to borrow a book from a fellow state legislator he barely knew. This man granted the request and thereafter was friendly to Franklin (who had soon afterward returned the book with a note expressing his appreciation). Empirical studies have shown this effect among relative acquaintances — one kindness often leads to another. See Meg Jay, *The Defining Decade*, and the original research she cites.

7. In an article in *U.S. News & World Report*, Robin Madell writes that "a nationwide survey conducted by Fairfield Inn & Suites revealed that 77 percent of adults are willing to help college graduates find work" (Robin Madell, "Networking 101 for New Grads," *U.S. News & World Report*, June 10, 2014, http://money.usnews.com/money/blogs/outside-voices-careers/2014/06/10/networking-101-for-new-grads (accessed April 15, 2015).

Trap 9: I've Got a Paycheck and Can Finally Live It Up!

1. See Kim Parker, "The Boomerang Generation: Feeling OK about Living with Mom and Dad," March 2012, Pew Research Center, www.pewsocialtrends.org/files/2012/03/PewSocialTrends-2012-BoomerangGeneration.pdf (accessed April 15, 2015).

2. For this and other information, see Reyna Gobel's helpful book, *CliffsNotes Graduation Debt*, 2nd ed. (New York: Houghton Mifflin Harcourt, 2014).

3. Before July 2006, federal student loans had variable rates that could change once a year on July 1. Today, all federal loans have fixed rates. But the interest rate at which federal loans are issued is revised annually. So you might have loans from your freshman year at 4 percent and loans from your sophomore year at 5 percent. If you have both subsidized and unsubsidized loans, you'll end up with one consolidated subsidized loan and one consolidated unsubsidized loan. But you'll still make just one payment. Your loan company will simply divide this payment between the subsidized and unsubsidized loans.

4. If your amount owed is $10,000–$19,999, it's a fifteen-year payoff; $20,000–$39,999, a twenty-year payoff; $40,000–$59,999, a twenty-five-year payoff; $60,000 and higher, a thirty-year payoff. As we discussed in chapter 5, the longer the payoff, the lower your monthly payment but the more interest you end up paying in the long run. Assuming you *can* pay off your debt sooner, it's better to do so.

5. This concept is unpacked in Jim Newheiser and Elyse Fitzpatrick's wonderful book, *You Never Stop Being a Parent* (Phillipsburg, NJ: P&R, 2010).

6. "Average Annual Miles per Driver by Age Group," U.S. Department of Transportation, Federal Highway Administration, www.fhwa.dot.gov/ohim/onh00/bar8.htm (accessed April 15, 2015).

7. This $2,250 figure is after Emily's tithing and mandatory withholding but does not include the $150 monthly retirement withholding shown on the pie chart.

8. The exception to this advice is if your employer is a publically traded stock and you're able to purchase that stock at a discount. I was an IBM employee for three years. I could dedicate up to 10 percent of my salary to the purchase of IBM stock *at 15 percent below the market value.* If the stock price stayed flat, I'd still make a 15 percent gain. Such incentive programs are a good deal, but you want to remember to sell your stock after a year (so it's taxed at a lower rate than if you held it for less time). Otherwise, you'll soon have a lot of one company's stock, which exposes you to the risk of that stock going down in value.

9. U.S. Census Bureau, "Educational Attainment in the United States: 2013–Detailed Tables," www.census.gov/hhes/socdemo/education/data/cps/2013/tables.html (accessed April 15, 2015).

Conclusion: Be Free from Student Debt So You Can Live with Impact

1. See *ESV Study Bible*, note on Luke 16:4–7 (Wheaton, IL: Crossway, 2012).